FREE AND SUPER CHEAP CAMPING IN THE SOUTHWEST

TWO HUNDRED TWENTY FIVE 5-STAR CAMPSITES FOR NATIONAL FOREST CAMPING, BUREAU OF LAND MANAGEMENT, FEDERAL, STATE, COUNTY, RV CAMPING, TENT CAMPING, BOONDOCKING

FREE AND SUPER CHEAP CAMPING SERIES

BOOK SEVEN

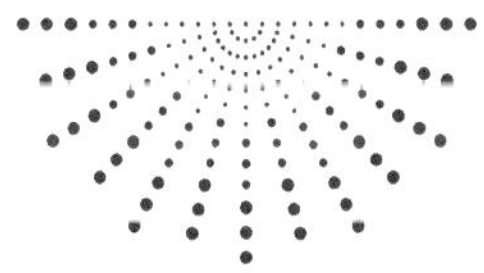

RICH SHIPLEY

WAYFARE ARTS LLC

Cover photo: Havasu Falls, Grand Canyon, Arizona

Photo credit: lucky-photo/Adobe Stock

FREE AND SUPER CHEAP CAMPING SERIES

The Free and Super Cheap Camping series is your passport to budget-friendly adventures across America's most beautiful public lands in:

COLORADO, UTAH, NEVADA, CALIFORNIA, OREGON, WASHINGTON, ARIZONA, NEW MEXICO

Each book features top-rated campsites, plus the tools and knowledge to help you discover thousands more. Whether you're camping in the mountains, by the sea, or in the desert, you'll find detailed information, GPS coordinates, maps, and tips to help you explore with confidence — all while keeping your travel costs low and your sense of freedom high.

SCAN OR CLICK BELOW TO SEE THE ENTIRE SERIES, AND START PLANNING YOUR NEXT CAMPING ADVENTURE.

Free and Super Cheap Camping Series: https://t2bk.com/ATT

CONTENTS

INTRODUCTION

Desert Vistas, Red Rock Canyons, Forested Peaks — Camp the Southwest Without Spending a Fortune

Free and Super Cheap Camping in the Southwest features 225 top-rated campsites across six stunning states: Arizona, New Mexico, Utah, Colorado, Nevada, and California.

This region is a land of extremes and wonders — where sandstone arches rise from the desert, alpine meadows sit above sweeping valleys, and remote hot springs and quiet canyons reward those willing to explore. Whether you're chasing winter sun or summer solitude, this guide will help you find beautiful, peaceful, and budget-friendly places to camp across some of the West's most iconic landscapes.

Until recently, I had been living and traveling full-time in various campers and RVs for almost seven years. For 95% of that time, I camped in great, free, or cheap places. If that sounds good, or if you want to learn about some beautiful places to camp and not spend a fortune just to be camped ridiculously close to your neighbor, follow along.

Hopefully, this book will give you some great ideas of where you might like to camp. By no means is this an exhaustive list! It's an excellent starter list, and at the end of the book, I will point you to resources with thousands of other great places to camp. More places than you could get to in a lifetime. For this book, I focus on some places where I, along with other campers, have given very high ratings. I won't be including RV parks or the higher-cost campgrounds. Those are not my thing, so I can't advise you on those places, but they can be found in the resources listed at the end of the book if you're interested.

Regarding the ratings, what I, or some other people, consider a highly rated campsite may or may not be your cup of tea, or it might not be suitable for your vehicle or your camping style. A variety of camp areas are available, ranging from sites suitable for tents only to those that can accommodate large RVs and motorhomes. Sites with amenities and sites with no facilities at all. A few sites may require a high clearance or a 4-wheel drive vehicle. Please read the listings, then conduct your own research to learn more about a potential camp area and better understand what to expect.

Each camping area listed will give you the name, whether it's free or low cost (at the time of writing), general location, GPS coordinates, the managing agency (forest service, BLM, etc.), and a brief description. **Again, once you've found something interesting, the next step in your planning would be to look up the campground by name or city/area on Google or one of the websites or apps listed at the end**

of this book. Please do your research! It's always best to check these to ensure you have the latest info in case of closures, fires, rough or washed-out roads, or whatever. You'll also find more reviews on these sites and info on cell service availability, elevation, etc.

Many sites listed are available on a first-come, first-served basis, while others can be reserved in advance. Here are the common reservation websites.

www.recreation.gov For most federal lands campgrounds.

www.reserveamerica.com for state and regional parks.

Do an internet search for county park reservations.

HOW TO USE THIS BOOK

For each campground listed, you will see links and QR codes. Depending on whether you are reading the paperback, Kindle, or a mobile device, you can click on a link or scan the QR code with your phone's camera. **This method allows you to see far more photos and detailed information than could ever be included in a book.**

Map: https://t2bk.com/AE

Here's a QR code example. Go ahead and try it out now.

AND FINALLY, A NOTE ABOUT THE PRICES LISTED

Most campgrounds listed are managed by the National Forest Service or the Bureau of Land Management. For campgrounds with two prices, the lower price applies to those with an annual or senior pass. Information on those passes is available at the end of this book.

INTERACTIVE MAP. SCROLL AND ZOOM ALL OF THE CAMPSITES IN THIS BOOK. CLICK THE LINK OR SCAN THE QR CODE

Maps: https://t2bk.com/ATS

Site numbers on the map correspond to page numbers in the book.

Ok, enough said…

LET'S GO CAMPING IN THE SOUTHWEST!

1

SOUTH CENTRAL COLORADO

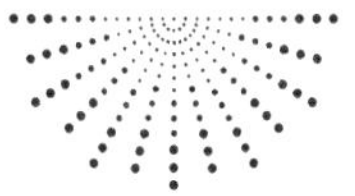

2. COMSTOCK CAMPGROUND - $10/$5

- Rio Grande National Forest
- FR-265
- Del Norte, CO
- GPS: 37.445, -106.362

Map: https://t2bk.com/AGW

COMSTOCK CAMPGROUND, located 18 miles southwest of Monte Vista in the Rock Creek Drainage, offers secluded camping. The campground has sites ranging from 35 to 40 feet in length. It's adjacent to the South Fork of Rock Creek, perfect for fishing. Hikers can explore trails like Alamosa River to Rock Creek Trail 703 and South Fork Rock Creek Trail 702, some of which are open to motorcycles and ATVs.

Facilities include tables, fire rings, and a vault toilet, but there's no water or trash service, so pack it in and out. Maneuvering large trailers might be challenging due to space constraints. The area is lightly used and beautifully tucked away, with a somewhat rocky and narrow access road.

Photos: https://t2bk.com/AGX

3. ZAPATA FALLS CAMPGROUND - $11/$5.50

- BLM
- Mosca, CO 81146
- Reservations: recreation.gov
- GPS: 37.6197, -105.5603

Map: https://t2bk.com/AGY

Zapata Falls Campground is tucked away among piñon pines, offering 23 sites across two loops: one dedicated to tent camping and the other accommodating RVs of all sizes. Facilities here include tables, tent pads, fire rings, food storage lockers, vault toilets, and trash bins, but you'll need to bring any required water. A new trail provides access to the South Zapata Creek Trail and the vast Sangre de Cristo Wilderness, while another path leads to the stunning Zapata Falls, just a half-mile hike away.

Photos: https://t2bk.com/AGZ

This campground is a vantage point for breathtaking views, overlooking the valley, the San Juan Mountains, the Great Sand Dunes National Park and Preserve, and the towering peaks of the Sangre de Cristo Mountain range. The area around Zapata Falls is rich in history and geology, perfect for those who love hiking, camping, mountain biking, and soaking in magnificent landscapes.

4. NORTH CRESTONE CREEK CAMPGROUND - $10/$5

- Rio Grande del Norte National Monument
- County Road U71
- Crestone, CO
- GPS: 38.016, -105.689

Map: https://t2bk.com/AHC

This campground, stretching along 0.7 miles of North Crestone Creek, offers 13 sites in a forested setting. Tucked among aspen, juniper, fir, and other trees that love the water's edge, it's a first-come, first-served area. The sites are spaced out enough to give each one a secluded wilderness feel. It's conveniently close to the town of Crestone. It's primarily suitable for tents or very small RVs and is close to the North Crestone Trail trailhead.

Peaceful and relaxing camping next to a mountain stream tumbling over boulders. The campground is quiet, with easy access to hiking trails and the nearby village of Crestone. There are clean vault toilets available. You'll also find free dry camping in this area. This is bear country, so store all of your food properly. And don't forget to pack some bug spray when you visit!

Photos: https://t2bk.com/AHD

5. BUFFALO PASS CAMPGROUND - $10/$5

- Rio Grande National Forest
- Colorado 114
- Saguache, CO
- GPS: 38.1859, -106.5182

Photos: https://t2bk.com/AHE

Buffalo Pass Campground sits within a quiet Ponderosa Pine grove, encircled by a lush grass meadow. This serene spot offers 19 spacious sites, including four that are pull-through, perfect for a variety of camping styles. Sites #16, 17, and 18 are located on a secluded spur without a turnaround point. The area blooms with wildflowers, enhancing the beauty of the area.

Facilities here are basic, with a vault toilet, picnic tables, and fire rings provided, but campers will need to bring their own water and pack out their trash. The terrain's gentle undulations mean some sites sit higher or lower, and some are a bit off-level. While primarily catering to vans, small RVs, and tents, a handful of spots can fit slightly larger vehicles. This campground offers a quiet retreat among the national forest's aspen and pines.

Photos: https://t2bk.com/AHF

6. VALLEY VIEW HOT SPRINGS - $15

- Campground
- 64393 County Road GG
- Moffat, CO
- Reservations required: (719) 256-4315
- GPS: 38.1922, -105.8155

Map: https://t2bk.com/AHG

Valley View Hot Springs offers 23 reservation-only campsites, providing a mix of vistas overlooking the valley and secluded spots among the trees. There are no pull-throughs, hook-ups, Generators, and fires are not allowed. What it lacks in conventional camping amenities, it more than makes up for with breathtaking views, clean air, and the serene environment. Plus, you get 24-hour access to the hot pools and ponds, though there's an additional fee for this.

The camping area is mainly open, but you can find some shaded areas. Each site comes with a picnic table. THE SPRINGS ARE CLOTHING-OPTIONAL, offering a unique, natural experience. Cabins are also available for rent. Valley View is truly a retreat into nature, offering peace, community, and a mix of social and private spaces among its thermal pools.

Photos: https://t2bk.com/AHH

7. RED CANYON CAMPGROUND - FREE

- City Park
- County Road F24
- Canon City, CO
- GPS: 38.5858, -105.2485

Maps: https://t2bk.com/AHI

A unique dispersed camping area surrounded by stunning red rock formations offers a one-of-a-kind experience. The site has vault toilets and fire rings. Some spots have picnic tables, but there's no water available. Located about 10.5 miles and a 20-minute drive north of town on Red Canyon Road (CR9), the area is open year-round and is sometimes nicknamed “discount Sedona.” It's an excellent choice for those looking to hike and scramble in a less crowded setting.

Photos: https://t2bk.com/AHJ

This place is perfect if you're looking for a hidden gem away from the usual tourist spots. The hiking is full of surprises, with each turn offering a new view of the constantly changing canyon walls. There's plenty to explore, with the scenery being beautiful and fun to navigate through rocks and arroyos. The canyon provides shade on warm days, and the rock formations are fantastic.

8. THE BANK CAMPGROUND - $7/$3.50

- BLM
- Shelf Road
- Canon City, CO
- GPS: 38.6279, -105.2255

Map: https://t2bk.com/AHK

Thanks to the fantastic climbing opportunities right next to the site, Bank Campground is popular with rock climbing enthusiasts. With access to nearly 1,000 bolted routes through the Cactus Cliff and Dark Side trails, it's a climber's paradise. The area is also great for hiking, mountain biking, horseback riding, and 4-wheel drive adventures. Perched above Shelf Road at 6,890 feet, the campground offers a great view of the surroundings.

This spot has 31 campsites with metal fire rings and picnic tables, as well as 2 group sites and 4 vault toilets. Other popular activities include visiting the Royal Gorge via the Royal Gorge Bridge, taking the Royal Gorge Train, hitting the hiking trails, or joining a rafting trip. The Arkansas River nearby is perfect for whitewater rafting and fishing. The sites are on the smaller side, mainly suited for tent camping. The Bank is not recommended for large trailers and RVs.

Maps: https://t2bk.com/AHL

9. THE CRAGS CAMPGROUND - $22/$11

- Pike-San Isabel National Forests & Cimarron and Comanche National Grasslands
- Teller County Road 62
- Divide, CO
- GPS: 38.871, -105.12

Map: https://t2bk.com/AHM

The Crags Campground has 17 spots perfect for tents or small RVs and trailers, potable water, and a vault toilet. Access is via a rough dirt road, unsuitable for large trailers. There's no trash pickup here, so you must take your garbage. You might not find water or a camp host outside the busy season.

This secluded spot is a gateway to stunning trails like the Crags and Devil's Playground, with the trailhead just a short walk from the campground. Plus, the Ring-the-Peak trail runs past the campground, adding to your hiking options. It's a serene, first-come, first-served campground where each site is nestled among trees, offering privacy and sometimes even a creek running right through.

Photos: https://t2bk.com/AHN

10. COVE CAMPGROUND - $22/$11

- Pike-San Isabel National Forests & Cimarron and Comanche National Grasslands
- County Road 387
- Lake George, CO
- Reservations: recreation.gov
- GPS: 38.909, -105.461

Map:https://t2bk.com/AHO

Tucked away in Eleven Mile Canyon by the South Platte River, Cove Campground is small and perfect for those who love fishing and rock climbing. It's a peaceful area with just four campsites available for tents or trailers up to 16 feet. Toilets, water, trash facilities, picnic tables, and fire rings. Reservations are a good idea on weekends or in the summer, as it can get busy.

There's direct access to the river for fishing or just splashing around. Good hiking in the area, too. The fishing here is renowned for being among the best trout fishing spots in the country. It can get busy on weekends, but it's worth the trip for the beautiful scenery and world-class fishing.

Photos: https://t2bk.com/AHP

11. LENHARDY CUTOFF DISPERSED CAMPING - FREE

- Pike-San Isabel National Forest
- Lenhardy Cutoff
- Buena Vista, CO
- GPS: 38.8581, -106.054

Map: https://t2bk.com/AHQ

Lenhardy Cutoff and its surrounding areas offer some fantastic dispersed camping sites. These spots have incredible views of the Collegiate Peaks and the Buena Vista area, making for a stunning backdrop. The campsites here are spacious and peaceful, perfect if you want to camp near Buena Vista. However, be prepared for a rough ride in, as the road has some steep and rocky sections. High-clearance vehicles are recommended for this terrain.

But for those who love hiking, there are numerous off-trail opportunities, like mountain climbing, and the Midland Mountain Bike Trail runs along the Lenhardy Cutoff. So, if you've got a vehicle that can handle rough roads, you're in for a treat with breathtaking mountain scenery and plenty of adventurous trails to explore.

Photos: https://t2bk.com/AHR

12. RASPBERRY GULCH DISPERSED CAMPING - FREE

- Pike-San Isabel National Forests
- FR-274A
- Nathrop, CO
- GPS: 38.7016, -106.1627

Map: https://t2bk.com/AHS

Raspberry Gulch is conveniently close to both Buena Vista and Salida. It's a picturesque area with plenty of space to park, and the views are amazing. Plenty of room and privacy here, too. Its location is perfect for exploring nearby towns like Salida and Buena Vista and is an excellent base for hiking adventures. The Collegiate Peaks are nearby, along with other trailheads in the area. A hike up Browns Creek to the falls is a highlight.

It's suitable for all sizes of camping rigs, with views of Mt. Princeton. Exit the highway on FR 270, and you'll find plenty of great spots for setting up camp along FR 270, 273, and 274. This vast area allows plenty of room to spread out, making it a top choice for many campers. It's highly recommended for anyone looking to enjoy this part of Colorado.

Photos: https://t2bk.com/AHT

13. FOREST ROAD 272 DISPERSED CAMPING - FREE

- Pike-San Isabel National Forests & Cimarron and Comanche National Grasslands
- FR-272
- Nathrop, CO
- GPS: 38.6933, -106.1355

Map: https://t2bk.com/AHU

There are lots of sites to choose from, and they're nicely spread out and suitable for any rig size. The road to get there is in pretty good shape and it's wide enough for vehicles to pass each other easily. The camping spaces are mostly level, with some offering full sun and others more shade. It's about a 25-minute drive to either Buena Vista or Salida.

The area is right under the Collegiate Peaks, offering fantastic scenery. There's a large network of forest service roads around, so you have many hiking and biking trail options. It's a beautiful and convenient place for dispersed camping, with mountains all around, lots of trails to explore, a waterfall hike at Brown's Creek, and the Colorado Trail nearby.

Photos: https://t2bk.com/AHV

14. BROWNS CREEK DISPERSED CAMPING - FREE

- Pike-San Isabel National Forest
- FR-272
- Nathrop, CO
- GPS: 38.6692, -106.1594

Map: https://t2bk.com/AHW

This is a hidden gem nestled along Brown's Creek, with plenty of large and private spots for camping, suitable for all sizes of rigs. The night sky here is a sight to behold, with stars and the Milky Way visible in all their glory! You can also explore the nearby Brown's Creek Trail, leading to a stunning waterfall.

This campground is part of the Pike-San Isabel National Forests & Cimarron and Comanche National Grasslands, which spans over three million acres across western Kansas and Colorado. You can expect diverse ecosystems, stunning scenery, and a wide range of recreational activities to enjoy in this area.

Photos: https://t2bk.com/AHX

15. BLUE MOUNTAIN CAMPGROUND - $17/$8.50

- Pike-San Isabel National Forests & Cimarron and Comanche National Grasslands
- Forest Road 244
- Lake George, CO
- Reservations: recreation.gov
- GPS: 38.9592, -105.3617

Map: https://t2bk.com/AHY

Blue Mountain Campground, with 21 campsites, is just a short drive from Lake George. It's perfect for those not hauling anything longer than 25 feet, sitting at an elevation of 8,200 feet. The basics are covered here with toilets, water, tables, and fire rings, making it a good choice for a getaway not too far west of Colorado Springs.

This spot offers quiet and privacy, with large sites spaced out nicely. You'll need to pack out your trash. The access road is in good shape. The area is good for activities like fishing, hiking, and off-roading. It's also a great base for exploring local attractions like the Florissant Fossil Beds, Pikes Peak, Cripple Creek, and more. There's a trail nearby that offers views over Eleven Mile Canyon.

Photos: https://t2bk.com/AHZ

16. HAPPY MEADOWS CAMPGROUND - $22/$11

- Pike-San Isabel National Forests & Cimarron and Comanche National Grasslands
- County Road 112
- Lake George, CO
- Reservations: recreation.gov
- GPS: 39.0146, -105.3623

Map: https://t2bk.com/AIA

Happy Meadows Campground is nestled by the South Platte River, close to Eleven Mile Reservoir and Eleven Mile Canyon. Excellent for fishing, tubing, and hiking. Seven reservable (5 days in advance) RV sites, each with a picnic table and a fire ring. Water and a vault toilet are on-site. It is just a short walk from the campsites to the beautiful South Platte River.

Lots of wildlife, and the area has seven mountains over 14,000 feet high, along with extensive trails for exploring. Fishing for trout here is world-class. Florissant Fossil Beds, with its fossils and petrified redwoods, is nearby, and both Eleven Mile Canyon and the Tarryall Valley offer scenic drives with breathtaking views.

Photos: https://t2bk.com/AIB

17. ROUND MOUNTAIN CAMPGROUND - $22/$11

- Pike-San Isabel National Forests & Cimarron and Comanche National Grasslands
- Forest Road 225
- Lake George, CO
- Reservations: recreation.gov
- GPS: 39.0302, -105.4336

Map: https://t2bk.com/AIC

Round Mountain Campground is a rustic campground close to Lake George, Eleven Mile Canyon, and Florissant Fossil Beds National Monument. Close to hiking, biking, fly fishing, and wildlife-watching spots. Sitting at 8,500 feet, the campground has 15 reservable sites nestled among ponderosa pines and young aspens.

Photos: https://t2bk.com/AID

The mild summer days and cool nights, courtesy of the high altitude, are perfect if you're looking to escape the heat. The changing aspens in the fall add a stunning golden hue to the landscape. Facilities include picnic tables, vault toilets, campfire rings, and a hand pump for water. This is a 'pack in, pack out' facility. The area is rich in wildlife and offers incredible stargazing opportunities.

18. SPRINGDALE CAMPGROUND - $22/$11

- Pike-San Isabel National Forests & Cimarron and Comanche National Grasslands
- Rampart Range Rd. (FR-300)
- Woodland Park, CO
- GPS: 38.997, -105.0243

Map: https://t2bk.com/AIG

Springdale Campground, a short drive from Woodland Park, along Rampart Range Road. It's a small place with 13 first come, first serve spots, so early birds get the sites. It's not ideal for large RVs. It has clean vault toilets, but remember to bring any water you will need. The campground has lovely shaded areas, and many sites offer plenty of privacy.

The area is also an easy ride from Colorado Springs and is excellent for wildlife spotting with deer, elk, and more nearby. It's a peaceful spot, perfect for a quiet getaway. Getting there involves a drive on mostly well-paved roads, though you will encounter a few rough patches and tight bends. If you plan to visit Rampart Reservoir nearby, your campground ticket will cover your parking fee at the lake. It's a popular spot, so arrive early to secure a site.

Photos: https://t2bk.com/AIH

19. RAMPART RANGE ROAD DISPERSED CAMPING - FREE

- Pike-San Isabel National Forests & Cimarron and Comanche National Grasslands
- Rampart Range Rd (FR-300)
- Woodland Park, CO
- GPS: 38.9757, -105.0088

Map:https://t2bk.com/AII

Beautiful and remote but still easy to reach. It has an excellent view of Pikes Peak. The air is fresh and clean, and the view is unforgettable. Just a 20-minute drive from Woodland Park, you have easy access to supermarkets and outdoor stores, and it's about 45 minutes from Colorado Springs.

The area has a selection of dispersed camping spots with breathtaking mountain views. It's peaceful and quiet, with lots of trails to explore. There are three side roads designated for dispersed camping. First-come, first-serve. There are no facilities, so pack out everything you bring in. The road to the campsite is a bit of a washboard, but it's worth the drive for the beautiful setting.

Photos: https://t2bk.com/AIJ

20. LOST PARK CAMPGROUND - $20/$10

- Pike-San Isabel National Forests & Cimarron and Comanche National Grasslands
- Lost Park Road (CR-56)
- Jefferson, CO
- GPS: 39.2848, -105.5073

Map; https://t2bk.com/AIK

Lost Park Campground, nestled 21 miles southeast of Jefferson by US 285 and CR 56, offers a getaway with 12 spots suitable for trailers up to 22 feet. At an elevation of 10,000 feet, it provides basic amenities like toilets, tables, water, and fire rings, but you'll need to pack out your trash since there's no service. Getting there involves roughly 20 miles of dirt road.

This campground is a serene haven with a stream teeming with Brook trout, perfect for anglers. It's an ideal retreat for anyone looking to unplug and soak in nature's beauty. The area has fantastic hiking trails catering to different skill levels, offering solitude and a chance to truly relax. Remember to be bear-aware and leave no trace behind. With excellent fishing and secluded hiking spots, it's a slice of paradise.

Photos: https://t2bk.com/AIL

21. KENOSHA PASS DISPERSED CAMPING - FREE

- Pike-San Isabel National Forests & Cimarron and Comanche National Grasslands
- FR-126
- Jefferson, CO
- GPS: 39.4171, -105.7526

Map: https://t2bk.com/AIM

Kenosha Pass is a gateway to some fantastic trails. It connects to the Colorado Trail, stretching outside Denver to Durango. The trail runs by both the Kenosha Pass and Kenosha East Campgrounds. If you're into fall colors, this area is a must-see with its vibrant aspen trees.

The Kenosha Pass trailhead gets crowded with folks coming to see the autumn leaves from late September to early October. This location is super quiet, and the campsites are beautiful and spacious. You'll have plenty of privacy, great views, and no road noise or light pollution. The campsites are nestled in a small valley of aspens, making it a peaceful and picturesque spot to camp.

Photos: https://t2bk.com/AIN

22. KITE LAKE CAMPGROUND - $15/$7.50

- Pike-San Isabel National Forests & Cimarron and Comanche National Grasslands
- County Road 8
- Alma, CO
- GPS: 39.3287, -106.1287

Map: https://t2bk.com/AIQ

Kite Lake Campground, on County Road 8, is small with just 5 campsites, mainly suited for tents rather than trailers. You'll find the basics here, like fire rings, tables, and outhouse toilets, but you'll need to bring water and pack out your trash. It's a first-come, first-served deal, and the views are worth it. You'll want a heavy-duty truck or 4x4 to get there; a regular car might struggle.

The area is gorgeous, with lots of great hikes, but it does get busy, especially in the mornings when people come to tackle the nearby 14ers. If you aim to hike those peaks, staying the night before is a good idea since it gets packed in the summer. Remember to pack warm clothes, even in the summer months. And the altitude here is no joke, so take it easy and enjoy the stunning scenery.

Photos; https://t2bk.com/AIR

23. GUANELLA PASS CAMPGROUND - $23/$11.50

- Arapaho National Forest
- Guanella Pass Road
- Georgetown, CO
- Reservations: recreation.gov
- GPS: 39.6117, -105.7176

Map: https://t2bk.com/AIY

Guanella Pass Campground is about 7 miles south of Georgetown, on the South Fork of Clear Creek along the Guanella Pass Scenic Byway. Note that nights can get chilly at 10,900 feet. It's an excellent place for hiking and fishing. It's more suited for tents and smaller trailers, as the byway is NOT recommended for larger RVs. Sites have tent pads, picnic tables, fire rings, and a charcoal grill. There's potable water, vault toilets, and trash dumpsters.

The campground is popular, so booking a spot ahead is a good idea. The area is just amazing, with a gorgeous creek. The sites are spacious and spread out, giving you the sense of having a little piece of the woods. It's well-kept, and the whole area is peaceful and beautiful—a great choice if you're looking to unwind and enjoy some stunning natural scenery.

Photos: https://t2bk.com/AIZ

24. LAKEVIEW CAMPGROUND - $27/$13.50

- Pike-San Isabel National Forests & Cimarron and Comanche National Grasslands
- CR-24
- Twin Lakes, CO
- GPS: 39.098, -106.3622

Map: https://t2bk.com/AJA

In the Twin Lakes area, Lakeview Campground is a developed campground amidst ponderosa pines and sage at 9,500 feet. Situated between Mt. Elbert Forebay and Twin Lakes, it provides easy access to the scenic Twin Lakes Reservoir and the towering Mount Elbert. Each site comes with a picnic table and a campfire ring. The campground offers vault toilets and trash collection, but as of this writing, there is no water available.

Good access to Twin Lakes, Leadville & Buena Vista. Incredible lake and mountain views and a clean and peaceful environment. Hiking and biking trails, fly fishing, rafting, and boating can be found nearby. The views around are stunning. See the previous listing for info on free camping in the area.

Photos: https://t2bk.com/AJB

25. BUFFALO SPRINGS CAMPGROUND - $22/$11

- Pike-San Isabel National Forests & Cimarron and Comanche National Grasslands
- FR-431
- Fairplay, CO
- Reservations: recreation.gov
- GPS: 39.0324, -105.9856

Map: https://t2bk.com/AJC

Buffalo Springs Campground, just a bit south of Fairplay along FS 431, has 18 campsites. Each site has enough room for vehicles with a trailer limit of 30 feet. The campground has toilets, tables, water, and fire rings nicely spaced out for privacy. It's an excellent spot for anyone looking to enjoy outdoor activities like biking, hiking, or rock climbing, surrounded by a beautiful forest.

Mid-week stays are quiet, though it does pick up on weekends. The campground is located just a mile from the highway. Everything's kept clean, including the vault toilets, and there's a camp host on-site. Many hiking trails are nearby. The drive to Leadville via Weston Pass Road is scenic, and you're also close to Buena Vista and Breckenridge.

Photos: https://t2bk.com/AJD

26. BLODGETT CAMPGROUND - FREE

- White River National Forest
- Homestake Reservoir Rd.
- Red Cliff, CO
- GPS: 39.4725, -106.3664

Map: https://t2bk.com/AJE

Blodgett Campground, on Homestake Creek, is a small spot with just 6 campsites. Each campsite has picnic tables, fire rings, and a vault toilet. It's located under the impressive cliff faces of Blodgett Canyon, a favorite with rock climbers. Just across Blodgett Creek, you'll find the Blodgett Canyon Picnic Area. The campground can fit RVs or trailers up to 45 feet, but it's popular, so arriving early is best.

Photos: https://t2bk.com/AJF

The area offers stunning views and a peaceful atmosphere. A short walk takes you to the creek, where the fishing is good. There's another dispersed camping area further down the road with more spots, although it's a bit more challenging to access. This gorgeous location is near the top of the Rockies National Scenic Byway, offering incredible starry nights and the sounds of wildlife. The mountain views at dusk and in the morning are breathtaking.

27. TWIN LAKES VIEW DISPERSED CAMPING - FREE

- Pike-San Isabel National Forests & Cimarron and Comanche National Grasslands
- CR-24
- Twin Lakes, CO
- GPS: 39.101, -106.3617

Map: https://t2bk.com/AFZ

The Twin Lakes area is a gem in Colorado's high country, offering grand views of its stunning landscapes. From the pristine alpine lakes to the towering mountain peaks and the vibrant Aspens, it's a paradise for nature lovers. This area has numerous dispersed camping sites, many with a rock fire pit, incredible views, and good tree cover.

The views from these sites, especially overlooking Twin Lakes Reservoir and the surrounding mountains, are breathtaking. Starting in early June, wildflowers bloom around the site, adding to its beauty. It's an incredible spot with expansive views and a star-filled night sky.

Photos: https://t2bk.com/AJN

28. COUNTY ROAD 48 DISPERSED CAMPING - FREE

- Pike-San Isabel National Forests & Cimarron and Comanche National Grasslands
- CR-48
- Leadville, CO
- GPS: 39.2478, -106.359

Map: https://t2bk.com/AJO

Just south of Turquoise Lake, County Road 48 offers the nearest dispersed camping to Leadville. It's a well-liked spot, so be ready for some company and remember to camp responsibly by leaving no trace. The location is excellent for checking out Turquoise Lake and the Mt. Massive Wilderness Area. The views of Mt. Elbert from here are breathtaking. The road is gravel but generally okay for most vehicles and setups.

You'll find plenty of solar-friendly sites, and the backdrop of the mountains adds to the peaceful, quiet atmosphere. It's a great free camping option not far from town. A dump station and potable water are available at the Leadville Sanitation on Hwy 24, just opposite the San Isabelle Forest Ranger Station.

Photos: https://t2bk.com/AJP

2

SOUTHWESTERN COLORADO

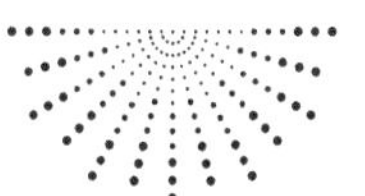

30. MUD SPRINGS CAMPGROUND - $10/$5

- BLM
- 16 5/10 Road
- Glade Park, CO
- GPS: 38.905, -108.7391

Map: https://t2bk.com/ALY

Mud Springs Campground, south of Grand Junction, is worth the drive. Twelve campsites on a first-come, first-serve basis. The road to there through Colorado Monument Park is breathtaking. Nestled in a grove of Aspen trees, the campground is beautiful, especially when the leaves change color in the fall. The aspens rustling in the breeze can make for a relaxing stay.

There's a host on-site, and the campground is just 5 miles from the Glade Park store. You'll find tables, fire pits, and water, and you'll need to pack out your trash. The bathrooms are newer, and you can choose from group or individual sites. There's also a free day-use picnic area. Enoch's Lake is just a short drive away if you're into fishing or kayaking. There are bike trails, bird watching, hiking, and nature trails to explore.

Photos: https://t2bk.com/ALZ

31. WARD LAKE CAMPGROUND - $22/$11

- Grand Mesa Uncompahgre and Gunnison National Forests
- FR-121
- Cedaredge, CO
- GPS: 39.0401, -107.9783

Map: https://t2bk.com/AMA

Ward Lake Campground, at an elevation of 10,200 ft, offers 27 campsites accommodating vehicles up to 45 ft. This campground winds along the shores of Ward Lake, nestled among spruce trees. You'll find some sites on the shore, others with lake views, and a few set back from the water. It's a popular spot, operating on a first-come, first-serve basis.

The campground provides easy access to the many lakes on the Grand Mesa, making it a prime location. This is mosquito country, so bring repellent. The natural beauty here is breathtaking, with the scent of pine and fresh air. It's a family-friendly place with clean vault toilets. Plus, it's excellent for fishing, hiking, and boating adventures.

Photos: https://t2bk.com/AMB

32. FLAT TOP OHV DESIGNATED CAMPSITES - FREE

- Gunnison Gorge National Conservation Area
- Flat Top Rd.
- Montrose, CO
- GPS: 38.522, -107.8594

Map: https://t2bk.com/AMC

Flat Top, set in the Gunnison Gorge National Conservation Area, is a desert area known for its mountain biking and off-highway vehicle (OHV) activities. Set between several national forests and near the Black Canyon of the Gunnison National Park, it's close to Montrose, Colorado. The Flat Top OHV Staging Area is a launchpad to about 75 miles of thrilling off-roading trails, including a spot for beginners, two play areas for OHVs, and a dedicated zone for motorcycles and ATVs. While OHV riding steals the show, the trails also attract mountain bikers looking for adventure against a stunning mountain backdrop.

Despite its basic setup as a dirt lot, the area is a good spot for camping, offering remarkable sunsets. The setting of the desert landscape and distant mountains creates a breathtaking scene, making Flat Top a unique place for outdoor enthusiasts seeking thrill and/or tranquility.

Photos: https://t2bk.com/AMD

33. LITTLE BEAR CAMPGROUND - $22/$11

- Grand Mesa Uncompahgre and Gunnison National Forests
- FR-116
- Cedaredge, CO
- GPS: 39.0345, -107.998

Map: https://t2bk.com/AME

Little Bear Campground is at 10,200 feet. There are 36 sites, including two that are wheelchair accessible. It's a mix here, with some sites being a good fit for RVs and others best for tents. It's first-come, first-serve, so no reservations. The area is forested with spruce trees. Potable water is available. There are fire pits and picnic tables at each site. Fishing, hiking, watersports.

The campground is close to many of Grand Mesa's 300 lakes, a visitor center, and the Crag Crest Trailhead. The setting is gorgeous—camping by a crystal blue alpine lake surrounded by pine-covered hills. Grand Mesa is unique, blending lake country and lush evergreen forests. Bring plenty of mosquito repellent! Be sure to take a drive to Crag Crest for spectacular views of the lakes.

Photos: https://t2bk.com/AMF

34. NORTH RIM CAMPGROUND - $20/$10

- Black Canyon of the Gunnison
- G74 Rd.
- Crawford, CO
- GPS: 38.5854, -107.7084

Map: https://t2bk.com/AMG

The North Rim campground is an excellent spot for those looking for a remote camping experience. There are 13 dispersed sites, so arrive early as they are first-come, first-served. The last 7 miles of the North Rim Road and the campground road are unpaved, so a vehicle with higher clearance is recommended. While services are limited, a vault toilet, a water spigot, bear boxes, trash, and tables are available. Some sites have a view of the canyon.

A trail from the campground goes along the rim and has some observation decks. If you want more views, a road just before the campground leads to various other view spots. Please use designated tent pads. The campground fills quickly during the summer, especially on weekends. The maximum combined length of an RV, car, and/or trailer is 22 feet.

Photos; https://t2bk.com/AMH

35. SOAP CREEK CAMPGROUND - $16/$8

- Grand Mesa Uncompahgre and Gunnison National Forests
- FR-721E
- Gunnison, CO 81230
- GPS: 38.5481, -107.3178

Map: https://t2bk.com/AMI

Soap Creek Campground has access to the southern trails of the West Elk Wilderness, including the Coal Mesa Trailhead on site. This serves as a gateway to a network of trails like 451.2 (Coal Mesa), 451, and 452. For those with horses, the campground provides convenient corrals and bins. With 21 campsites, it's a remote and clean location, offering spacious, shaded, and private sites, including some pull-throughs.

The views here are fantastic, and it's next to Soap Creek. The area has plenty of wildlife, including bears, deer, foxes, elk, and moose. Food must be kept inside a vehicle or hard-sided trailer. It's a beautiful spot that feels off the beaten path yet is conveniently close to town. The campground can get busy, but you might find it pleasantly quiet if you time it right. No Reservations. First Come, First Serve.

Photos: https://t2bk.com/AMJ

36. STEVENS CREEK CAMPGROUND - $20/$10

- Curecanti National Recreation Area
- U.S. 50
- Gunnison, CO 81230
- Reservations: recreation.gov
- GPS: 38.4878, -107.0916

Map: https://t2bk.com/AMK

Stevens Creek Campground is on the north shore at the eastern end of Blue Mesa Reservoir. Easy boating access to the reservoir. It's sunny and bright, with the aroma of sagebrush. It offers a quiet and convenient location on a beautiful high mesa. Clean pit toilets, nice tables and fire pits, and excellent sunset and lake views.

Photos: https://t2bk.com/AML

Nearby, you'll find Morrow Point Reservoir and Crystal Reservoir, both set among the steep cliffs of the Black Canyon. Stevens Creek provides waterfront sites and amenities like a picnic area, self-pay station, and drinking water. It's a perfect spot for stand-up paddleboarding, birdwatching, fishing, canoeing, and other water sports. The Neversink Trail, winding along the Gunnison River upstream of the Blue Mesa Reservoir, is great for hikers.

37. RED BRIDGE CAMPGROUND - $5/$2.50

- BLM
- Blue Mesa Road
- Powderhorn, CO
- GPS: 38.3239, -107.2267

Map: https://t2bk.com/AMM

Red Bridge Campground is located just off the Silver Thread National Scenic Byway. It's an excellent spot for fishing, sitting right on the Lake Fork of the Gunnison River. The area also offers access to the scenic Lake Fork Spur Drive. Its riverside location is an ideal place for a peaceful fishing getaway.

Photos: https://t2bk.com/AMN

The campground features 7 campsites and a restroom. Each campsite has a parking spot, a metal fire ring, and a picnic table. No potable water, so bring all that you'll need. The sites are mostly suited for tent or van camping, but there are a few that can accommodate larger rigs. It's a simple, rustic spot surrounded by trees, offering a quiet environment. At night, the sky presents an incredible display of stars.

38. BEAVER LAKE CAMPGROUND - $12/$6

- Grand Mesa Uncompahgre and Gunnison National Forests
- 5209 County Road 858
- Cimarron, CO
- GPS: 38.2502, -107.543

Map: https://t2bk.com/AMO

Beaver Lake Campground on Beaver Lake has 11 first-come, first-serve sites nestled under spruce trees, with some offering lake, meadow, and cliff views. The tent sites are more secluded. The lake is popular for fishing among both day users and campers. There's no drinking water available on-site, but it can be found a mile south at Silver Jack Campground. There are no nearby towns for provisions, so visitors should bring everything they need.

This small campground is set beside a beautiful lake frequented by ducks, beavers, and birds. Along with excellent fishing opportunities, there are nearby hiking and OHV trails. Facilities include very clean toilets. Access involves a long, winding gravel road, and there are good boondocking spots further up the road.

Photos: https://t2bk.com/AMP

39. SILVER JACK CAMPGROUND - $18/$9

- Grand Mesa Uncompahgre and Gunnison National Forests
- County Road 858
- Gunnison, CO 81230
- GPS: 38.2377, -107.5371

Map: https://t2bk.com/AMQ

Silver Jack Campground, with its 60 first-come, first-serve campsites, is nestled in a forest rich with aspens, a sprinkling of spruce trees, tall grass, and wildflowers. Wonderful campground in the aspen trees! Near the Silver Jack Reservoir is excellent for fishing and paddling, and there is a network of trails around the Cimarron Ridge, so there are plenty of outdoor activities. Campers have access to drinking water and vault toilets. There are no nearby communities for provisions, so bring everything you need.

This is bear country, so practice safe food storage. Sites have picnic tables and fire rings. The campground is well-maintained, with many sites enveloped in thick aspen forests providing privacy. There are numerous trails for hiking, cycling, and ATV riding in the area.

Photos: https://t2bk.com/AMR

40. LEDGES ROCKHOUSE CAMPGROUND - $5/$2.50

- BLM
- BB36 Road
- Nucla, CO
- GPS: 38.235, -108.3692

Map: https://t2bk.com/AMS

Ledges Rockhouse Campground is a peaceful spot by the San Miguel River. There is space for both RVs and tents, with cabanas, picnic areas, grills, restrooms, and a boat ramp, all nestled among cottonwood trees. The access road can get tricky in wet weather, turning slick and potentially challenging to navigate.

This secluded campground sees fewer visitors, making it a perfect getaway if you're looking to escape the hustle and bustle. It is a public road, so if the fence/gate is closed, close it behind you. It's a great place if you enjoy fishing, bird watching, or just soaking in the quiet. Wildlife, including bears and mountain lions, might wander through at night, so it's wise to watch pets and children closely.

Photos: https://t2bk.com/AMT

41. CADDIS FLATS CAMPGROUND - FREE

- BLM
- CO-145
- Placerville, CO
- GPS: 38.0277, -108.0916

Map: https://t2bk.com/AMU

Cadis Flats Campground is a small campground between the Scenic Byway and the San Miguel River, and is in a transition zone from forest to high desert scenery. It features three developed campsites, one of which includes a cabana. The campground also provides four parking areas for large RVs and boat trailers. You'll find concrete picnic tables and fire pits beside the picturesque San Miguel River. Clean vault toilet, but no drinking water. There's a hand-carry boat launch.

There are only a few designated sites, but the dirt parking area offers space for additional campers. The campground is just 18 miles from Telluride. It's a well-maintained BLM site that's perfect for river-side camping. It's close to towns like Telluride, Ridgeway, and Silverton. Great dark sky stargazing offers a spectacular view of the galaxy.

Photos: https://t2bk.com/AMV

42. MARY E CAMPGROUND - $18/$9

- Grand Mesa Uncompahgre and Gunnison National Forests
- CR-63L
- Telluride, CO
- GPS: 37.94, -107.8972

Map: https://t2bk.com/AMW

Nestled in a dense aspen grove and close to the South Fork of the San Miguel River near Telluride, Mary E Campground offers 20 spots on a first-come, first-served basis. It's suitable for tents and smaller RVs or trailers, with picnic tables, fire rings, and grills at each site. You'll find vault toilets and a place for your trash, but remember to bring any water you need. During the season, the campground host sells firewood.

The area is excellent for outdoor activities, from fishing and hiking to mountain biking and wildlife viewing. For those ready for a taste of civilization, the historic town of Telluride is just a short drive away, packed with shops, eateries, and local attractions. Despite its peaceful nights under starry skies, you might hear the sound of passing trucks in the daytime.

Photos: https://t2bk.com/AMX

43. LIZARD HEAD PASS DISPERSED CAMPING - FREE

- Grand Mesa Uncompahgre and Gunnison National Forests
- County Road A63
- Ophir, CO
- GPS: 37.8112, -107.9057

Map: https://t2bk.com/AMY

Lizard Head Pass, at just above 10,000 feet, is a small area with stunning views of the mountains. It's known for its meadows dotted with wildflowers. The drive from Telluride to here is gorgeous, especially when the aspens turn a brilliant yellow in the fall. There's a rest stop across the road with a pit toilet and a garbage dumpster for convenience. You'll find great hiking trails from your campsite, including the Lizard Head Pass trail across the road.

The night sky here is a real treat, with clear views in every direction and breathtaking sunrises and sunsets. It's an incredibly picturesque spot, ideal for biking or hiking. The views are amazing, and the fresh air and hiking are top-notch. Trails leading into the Lizard Head wilderness are beautiful in the summer, covered in wildflowers.

Photos: https://t2bk.com/AMZ

44. ANVIL DISPERSED CAMPING - FREE

- San Juan National Forest
- FR-585
- Silverton, CO
- GPS: 37.821, -107.7192

Map: https://t2bk.com/ANA

This spot is a gem tucked away in the San Juan Mountains along Mineral Creek. You'll be falling asleep to the gentle sounds of the creek here. The area doesn't have designated campsites, but there's plenty of space available, with some spots right by the creek, and the sounds can be enjoyed all night. The areas are large enough to accommodate bigger rigs as well.

The location is perfect, set in a stunning environment with amazing views and a beautiful creek as well. It's close to Silverton, and it can get busier on the weekends, but the beauty and tranquility of the place make it worth the visit.

Photos: https://t2bk.com/ANB

45. KENDALL CAMPGROUND - FREE

- San Juan National Forest
- FR-585
- Silverton, CO
- GPS: 37.8203, -107.7135

Map: https://t2bk.com/ANC

This is a gorgeous location for dispersed camping, with a stunning stream running through it. While no designated sites exist, you'll find plenty of nice flat spots to set up camp. Plus, pit toilets are available, and it's a great spot for larger rigs. Beautiful peaks surround the area, and there are many great hiking trails to explore, including some that lead up to mountain lakes. Plus, it's very close to Silverton, so you can easily access amenities.

The cell signal is decent here, and you'll be within easy reach of many popular off-road trails. You'll also enjoy amazing views of the surrounding mountains. Head into Silverton and ride the Silverton-Durango Train!!

Photos: https://t2bk.com/AND

46. BRADFIELD CAMPGROUND - $8/$4

- San Juan National Forest
- Bradfield Recreation Road
- Cahone, CO
- GPS: 37.6578, -108.7377

Map; https://t2bk.com/ANG

Bradfield Campground, 30 miles northwest of Dolores in the Dolores River Canyon below McPhee Dam, is a large area with 22 campsites. They're all available on a first-come, first-serve basis. The campground offers convenient access to a boat ramp and trailer parking, which becomes quite busy during the rafting season on the Dolores River, particularly around Memorial Day weekend.

Amenities include potable water, trash pickup, vault toilets, covered picnic tables, and fire grates. From September to May, these services are either limited or unavailable. This campground is a great find, not too far off the beaten path and right next to the Dolores River. The sites are generously spread out, making it a peaceful and quiet location. Plus, there's a nice deep swimming hole to enjoy. It's a perfect spot with lots of space to relax and soak in the natural beauty.

Photos: https://t2bk.com/ANH

47. MADDEN PEAK ROAD DISPERSED CAMPING - FREE

- San Juan National Forest
- FR-316
- Hesperus, CO
- GPS: 37.3476, -108.2016

Photos: https://t2bk.com/ANI

Looking for a free camping option near Mesa Verde National Park? This spot, about 14 miles from the park, is a good choice. The lower section has several campsites that are accessible for most vehicles. It's especially handy for larger vehicles because some of the sites are designed for pull-through access, making it easier to set up camp.

Photos: https://t2bk.com/ANJ

The campsites here are nicely spaced out, so you won't be too close to your neighbors, reducing the chance of noise disturbances. It's a peaceful setting. Keep in mind, though, that the sites further up the hill are better for tent camping only. It’s a good area for different types of campers, whether you're in a big rig or pitching a tent.

48. SAULS CREEK DISPERSED CAMPING - FREE

- San Juan National Forest
- CR-527
- Bayfield, CO
- GPS: 37.2432, -107.5512

Map: https://t2bk.com/ANK

This National Forest area near Bayfield, Colorado, has an abundance of trails set in breathtaking scenery. The campsites are well spread out, offering plenty of privacy for a peaceful camping experience. It's pretty easy to get to, and you're guaranteed tranquility.

When you arrive, take a moment to look at the big map; it's your gateway to exploring numerous hiking and mountain biking trails right from your campsite. There are lots of great spots all along these roads. Whether you're into trail running, mountain biking, or just lounging in a chair soaking up the beauty, this place is paradise. There's a lot of wildlife here – bears, mountain lions, and more call this place home. If you love clear blue skies, towering trees, and the scent of pine, you might find it hard to leave.

Photos: https://t2bk.com/ANL

49. TURKEY SPRINGS ROAD DISPERSED CAMPING - FREE

- BLM
- FR-629
- Pagosa Springs,
- GPS: 37.3334, -107.127

Map: https://t2bk.com/ANO

Fantastic boondocking spot near Pagosa Springs. The area is stunning, offering peace and quiet, well-maintained roads, and spacious campsites. It's an excellent place for shaded and easy mountain biking trails. The Turkey Springs mountain bike trail system is a highlight here, featuring 14 interconnected single-track routes for non-motorized use.

With over 30 miles of trails spread across Turkey Springs, Brockover Mesa, and Martinez Creek, bikers have plenty of loop options starting from various trailheads. There's a variety of campsites sites available, suitable for rigs of any size, and easy access to a network of gravel forest roads and ATV trails for more exploration. You can spend an hour or a day riding without retracing your steps.

Photos: https://t2bk.com/ANP

50. WEST FORK SAN JUAN RIVER DISPERSED CAMPING - FREE

- San Juan National Forest
- West Fork Road
- Pagosa Springs, CO
- GPS: 37.45, -106.9108

Map: https://t2bk.com/ANQ

There are only a few spots here, just a few that are down the road past a paid campground, which is quite nice itself. The area has beautiful views and is easy to get to, but it might be tight for larger rigs. This place is ideal if you have a smaller trailer or a tent. The road is well-maintained. And if you're into fishing, the river is just a quick walk away.

As you head in, you'll see the paid campground first, but keep going, and you'll come to several dispersed camping areas. Some spots have fire pits, river access, and room for big rigs. The second bridge, which marks the start of the dispersed camping, is about 2.2 miles from the main road. Also, for hikers, the trailhead to Rainbow Hot Springs is at the end of this road.

Photos: https://t2bk.com/ANR

51. RIVERS END CAMPGROUND - $18/$9

- Grand Mesa Uncompahgre and Gunnison National Forests
- County Road 742
- Almont, CO
- GPS: 38.8584, -106.5657

Map: https://t2bk.com/ANS

Rivers End Campground sits at the north end of Taylor Park Reservoir, a prime spot for fishing. There's a trail-head for Matchless Trail on site, complete with parking. It's also a great starting point for anyone into four-wheel driving, mountain biking, enduro biking, or horseback riding. The campground has 15 spots available on a first-come, first-serve basis. Heavy usage, so arrive early.

Great for activities like fishing and boating on the lake or the Taylor River or exploring the mountains by foot, bike, or motorized vehicles. You'll have 360° views of the mountains west of the Collegiate Range. There's no shade or secluded spots, but you're never far from the water. Facilities are basic but include everything you need, like vault toilets, a hand pump for water, fire rings, and tables.

Photos: https://t2bk.com/ANT

52. IRON CITY CAMPGROUND - $22/$11

- Pike-San Isabel National Forests & Cimarron and Comanche National Grasslands
- CR-292
- Nathrop, CO
- GPS: 38.7085, -106.3359

Map: https://t2bk.com/ANU

Iron City Campground, in Chalk Creek Canyon, is a favorite among ATV enthusiasts. It's a first-come, first-served campground with 15 available sites. The area is known for its scenic wooded campsites and proximity to Chalk Creek, with a wooded setting for campers. During peak season, water and vault toilets are available. You'll find stunning mountain views and a quick drive to the fascinating Saint Elmo ghost town.

The Iron City cemetery tells the history of the area's early settlers and miners, complete with interpretive signage. It's best suited for rigs shorter than 29 feet due to the smaller parking spaces. The region is a haven for outdoor activities like hiking, biking, and four-wheeling. For those using GPS: avoid the right fork off Chalk Creek Road and, instead, head left towards St Elmo to avoid a tricky, potentially muddy path.

Photos: https://t2bk.com/ANV

53. HARTMAN ROCKS DESIGNATED DISPERSED CAMPING - FREE

- BLM
- County Road 32C
- Gunnison, CO
- GPS: 38.4989, -106.9483

Map: https://t2bk.com/ANW

Hartman Rocks Recreation Area near Gunnison sprawls over 14,000 acres and is a haven for outdoor enthusiasts. With 45 miles of singletrack trails and 45 miles of roads, plus 50 designated dispersed campsites and numerous climbing spots, it's an adventure playground with epic million-dollar views.

The trails are for mountain biking, dirt biking, hiking, and trail running, while 16 miles of roads are groomed for cross-country skiing in the winter, including classic and skate skiing, and some single-track trails are groomed as winter singletrack for fat biking. All sites are first come, first serve. No fees. No hookups! No potable water or developed facilities.

Photos: https://t2bk.com/ANX

3

CENTRAL UTAH

HOLEY LAND, ARCHES, MOAB, CANYONLANDS, LA SAL MOUNTAINS

55. WILLOW SPRINGS DESIGNATED CAMPING - $15

- UtahRaptor State Park
- Willow Springs Trail
- Moab, UT 84532
- GPS: 38.6968, -109.6981

Maps: https://t2bk.com/RP

Willow Springs Designated Camping is located within UtahRaptor State Park near Moab, Utah. It offers a desert setting surrounded by sandstone mesas, slick rock, and scattered juniper trees. The area is popular with mountain bikers and off-road enthusiasts, with easy access to the nearby Willow Springs Road OHV routes and the Klondike Bluffs trail system. There are no formal hiking trails from the campsites, but the open landscape allows for wandering and exploring. Wildlife sightings may include lizards, jackrabbits, and a variety of desert birds.

The camping area includes designated sites marked along Willow Springs Road, each with space for tents, vans, or small RVs. There are no hookups, potable water, or restrooms, so you must be fully self-contained and pack out all waste. Camping is first-come, first-served.

Photos: https://t2bk.com/RQ

56. BUCKBOARD CAMPGROUND - $20/$10

- Manti-La Sal National Forest
- North Creek
- Monticello, UT 84535
- GPS: 37.881, -109.449

Maps: https://t2bk.com/RR

Buckboard Campground is in Manti-La Sal National Forest at about 9,500 feet elevation, surrounded by aspen, spruce, and fir trees that provide plenty of shade and a cool, mountain atmosphere. The area is near the top of the Wasatch Plateau, offering access to scenic drives, hiking, fishing, and wildlife viewing. Nearby Skyline Drive and local trails connect to alpine lakes and meadows, where visitors often see deer, elk, and various bird species.

The campground offers ten single sites, each with a picnic table, fire ring, and two group sites. Vault toilets and drinking water are available during the summer season. Sites can accommodate tents, trailers, and small to medium RVs. Some sites are reservable, and others are on a first-come, first-served basis. The campground typically operates from late spring through early fall.

Photos: https://t2bk.com/RS

57. BLM 144 DISPERSED CAMPING - FREE

- BLM
- BLM-144
- Crescent Junction, UT
- GPS: 38.8788, -109.8083

Maps: https://t2bk.com/RT

BLM 144 Dispersed Camping is located near Crescent Junction, Utah, in a wide-open desert landscape marked by red rock mesas, sandy flats, and scattered juniper and sagebrush. The area offers broad views of the desert and distant La Sal Mountains. The open terrain is great for exploration on foot, and the site is popular with off-road enthusiasts due to its proximity to nearby dirt roads and jeep routes. Wildlife such as jackrabbits, lizards, and ravens are commonly seen.

Camping is dispersed without designated sites, facilities, or potable water. Visitors must be fully self-contained and pack out all waste. Tents and RVs are welcome, and camping is free on a first-come, first-served basis. This remote location offers a quiet, rugged desert camping experience.

Photos: https://t2bk.com/RU

58. BLACK RIDGE AREA DESIGNATED CAMPSITES - FREE

- BLM
- Yellow Circle Rd.
- Moab, UT 84532
- GPS: 38.429, -109.4215

Maps: https://t2bk.com/RV

Black Ridge Area Designated Campsites are located near Moab, Utah, on BLM land surrounded by red rock cliffs, desert mesas, and open sagebrush flats. The area offers stunning views of nearby canyons and access to a network of jeep trails and mountain biking routes. The open landscape provides plenty of space for exploring on foot. Wildlife sightings may include lizards, desert cottontails, and a variety of raptors soaring overhead.

Six designated campsites are marked along the access road. They provide space for tents, vans, or small RVs. This area is not suitable for big RVs. There are no facilities, vault toilets, or potable water, so campers must pack all supplies and dispose of waste. Sites are available on a first-come, first-served basis.

Photos: https://t2bk.com/RW

59. DALTON WELLS ROAD DESIGNATED CAMPING - $15

- UtahRaptor State Park
- Dalton Wells Rd.
- Moab, UT 84532
- GPS: 38.7112, -109.7033

Maps: https://t2bk.com/RX

Dalton Wells Road Designated Camping is within Utahraptor State Park near Moab, Utah. This rugged desert setting is surrounded by sandstone mesas, slick rock, and scattered juniper trees. The area is popular with mountain bikers, hikers, and off-road enthusiasts, with access to the Klondike Bluffs trail system and numerous OHV routes. This area is excellent for exploration and photography. Wildlife such as lizards, jackrabbits, and ravens are commonly seen.

The camping area has designated, marked sites along Dalton Wells Road, with space for tents, vans, or small RVs. It is not suitable for large RVs. There are no hookups, vault toilets, or potable water, so campers must be self-contained and pack out all waste. Sites are available on a first-come, first-served basis.

Photos: https://t2bk.com/RY

60. BRIDE CANYON DESIGNATED DISPERSED CAMPSITES - FREE

- BLM
- Gemini Bridges Road
- Moab, UT 84532
- GPS: 38.6118, -109.667

map https://t2bk.com/RZ

Bride Canyon Designated Dispersed Campsites are located near Moab, Utah, on BLM land surrounded by dramatic red rock formations, desert mesas, and sandy washes. The area is quiet, remote, with wide-open views and a rugged desert atmosphere. The surrounding terrain is excellent for hiking, photography, and exploration on foot. Visitors may spot wildlife such as mule deer, lizards, and various desert birds.

The designated campsites are spaced along the access road and marked for tents, vans, or small RVs. There are no facilities, vault toilets, or potable water, so campers must be self-sufficient and pack out all waste. Camping is available on a first-come, first-served basis.

Photos: https://t2bk.com/SA

61. SOUTH TEMPLE WASH DISPERSED CAMPING - FREE

- BLM
- Temple Mt. Rd.
- Green River, UT 84525
- GPS: 38.6548, -110.6585

Maps: https://t2bk.com/SB

South Temple Wash Dispersed Camping is south of Green River, Utah, in a rugged desert landscape of sandstone cliffs, narrow canyons, and sandy washes. The area is set within the San Rafael Swell, offering striking red rock scenery and a sense of remoteness. There are no formal hiking trails, but the surrounding terrain is excellent for exploring on foot, rock scrambling, and photography. Wildlife sightings may include lizards, jackrabbits, and occasional mule deer or desert bighorn sheep.

Camping is dispersed without designated sites, vault toilets, or potable water. You must be fully self-contained and pack out all trash and waste. Both tents and RVs are welcome. The ground is mostly sandy and rocky. Camping is first-come, first-served. South Temple is a beautiful and peaceful desert escape.

Photos: https://t2bk.com/SC

62. WILLOW FLAT (ISLAND IN THE SKY) CAMPGROUND - $15/$7.50

- Canyonlands National Park
- Green River Overlook Rd.
- Moab, UT 84532
- GPS: 38.3841, -109.8889

Maps: https://t2bk.com/SD

Willow Flat Campground is located in the Island in the Sky district of Canyonlands National Park, Utah, perched on a mesa with stunning views of the surrounding canyons and distant La Sal Mountains. The area is characterized by pinyon pine, juniper, and desert scrub, providing minimal shade in a rugged high-desert setting. Several scenic overlooks, including the famous Green River Overlook, are within walking distance, and nearby trails offer excellent opportunities for hiking and photography. Wildlife like lizards, chipmunks, and birds are often seen around the campground.

The campground has twelve first-come, first-served sites, each with a picnic table and fire ring. Vault toilets are available, but there is no potable water. Sites accommodate tents and small RVs, making this a quiet and scenic base for exploring the park.

Photos: https://t2bk.com/SE

63. HAMBURGER ROCK CAMPGROUND - $15/$7.50

- BLM
- Lock Hart Road
- Moab, UT 84532
- GPS: 38.192, -109.6697

Maps: https://t2bk.com/SF

Hamburger Rock Campground is located near Moab, Utah, on BLM land surrounded by striking red rock formations, desert slickrock, and scattered juniper trees. Named for the distinctive rock outcrop resembling a hamburger, the area offers a scenic, rugged desert setting. You can explore the nearby rock formations and open desert on foot. The area is popular with climbers, photographers, and those seeking a quiet base near Canyonlands National Park and Indian Creek. Wildlife sightings may include lizards, jackrabbits, and ravens.

The campground has several designated sites, each with a picnic table and fire ring. Vault toilets are available, but there is no potable water. Campsites are first-come, first-served and can accommodate tents and small RVs.

Photos: https://t2bk.com/SG

64. LOCKHART ROAD DISPERSED CAMPING - FREE

- BLM
- Lock Hart Road
- Moab, UT 84532
- GPS: 38.1825, -109.668

Maps: https://t2bk.com/SJ

Lockhart Road Dispersed Camping is near Moab, Utah, along a remote stretch of desert surrounded by red rock cliffs, mesas, and rugged canyons. The area offers expansive views and quiet, off-the-grid camping, making it popular with overlanders, off-roaders, and those looking to explore nearby Lockhart Basin or the Canyonlands backcountry. The area is great for exploration, photography, and wildlife viewing, with lizards, jackrabbits, and occasional mule deer spotted in the area.

Camping is dispersed with no designated sites, vault toilets, or potable water. Campers must be self-sufficient, packing in all supplies and packing out waste. Tents and RVs are welcome, though the terrain is mostly rocky and uneven. Camping is free on a first-come, first-served basis.

Photos: https://t2bk.com/SK

65. GEMINI BRIDGES ROAD DESIGNATED CAMPSITES - FREE

- BLM
- Mill Canyon Rd. (BLM 215)
- Moab, UT 84532
- GPS: 38.7114, -109.7271

Maps: https://t2bk.com/SL

Gemini Bridges Road Designated Campsites are located near Moab, Utah, along a scenic red rock corridor popular with off-roaders, mountain bikers, and hikers. The area features towering sandstone cliffs, desert mesas, and slickrock, with easy access to the famous Gemini Bridges rock formation. Visitors often explore the nearby landscape on foot or by bike. Wildlife such as lizards, desert cottontails, and birds of prey are common in the area.

The designated campsites are spaced along Gemini Bridges Road and marked for use, providing space for tents, vans, or small RVs. There are no hookups, vault toilets, or potable water, so campers must be self-contained and pack out all waste. Camping is first-come, first-served.

Photos: https://t2bk.com/SM

66. TEMPLE TOWNSITE CAMPGROUND - $15/$7.50

- BLM
- Temple Mountain Rd.
- Green River, UT 84525
- GPS: 38.657, -110.6617

Maps: https://t2bk.com/SN

Temple Townsite Campground is located near Green River, Utah, in a quiet desert setting surrounded by sandstone cliffs, open flats, and scattered juniper and sagebrush. The area is a peaceful base for exploring the San Rafael Swell and nearby canyons. The surrounding terrain offers opportunities for walking, rock scrambling, and photography. Campers may encounter wildlife such as lizards, mule deer, and various desert birds.

The campground features several designated sites, each with a picnic table and fire ring. Vault toilets are available, but there is no potable water, so campers must bring their own supplies. Sites accommodate tents, trailers, and small RVs. Camping operates on a first-come, first-served basis.

Photos: https://t2bk.com/SO

67. OOWAH CAMPGROUND - $10/$5

- Manti-La Sal National Forest
- Oowah Campground Road
- Moab, UT 84532
- GPS: 38.5019, -109.2732

Maps: https://t2bk.com/SP

Oowah Campground is in the Manti-La Sal National Forest near Moab, Utah, at about 8,800 feet elevation. It's a cool mountain escape surrounded by aspen, fir, and spruce trees. The campground is beside Oowah Lake, a small alpine lake popular for fishing and offering a beautiful and peaceful atmosphere. Nearby trails provide access for hiking and mountain biking through the La Sal Mountains, with scenic views and chances to spot wildlife such as deer, marmots, and a variety of songbirds.

The campground has eleven single sites, each with a picnic table, fire ring, and grill. Vault toilets are available, and drinking water is provided during summer. Sites are suitable for tents, small RVs, vans, truck campers, etc. Some campsites can be reserved in advance, others are first-come, first-served. The campground typically operates from late spring through fall.

Photos: https://t2bk.com/SQ

68. CRYSTAL GEYSER DISPERSED CAMPING - FREE

- BLM
- Little Valley Rd.
- Green River, UT 84525
- GPS: 38.9379, -110.135

Maps: https://t2bk.com/SR

Crystal Geyser Dispersed Camping is located just south of Green River, Utah, along the banks of the Green River near the unique cold-water Crystal Geyser. The area offers a mix of sandy flats, cottonwood trees, and desert scrub, with expansive views of the river and surrounding cliffs. Explore the riverbanks and nearby geological features. The geyser erupts irregularly, adding quite a distinctive feature to the area. Wildlife such as waterfowl, lizards, and desert songbirds are commonly seen.

There are no designated sites, vault toilets, or potable water. You'll need to be self-contained and pack out all waste. Both tents and RVs are welcome. Camping is free and available on a first-come, first-served basis.

Photos: https://t2bk.com/ST

69. LONE MESA CAMPGROUND - $20/$10

- BLM
- Dubinky Well Rd.
- Moab, UT 84532
- GPS: 38.6431, -109.8183

Maps: https://t2bk.com/SU

Lone Mesa Campground is near Moab, Utah, on BLM land, offering a high desert setting with sweeping views of mesas, canyons, and distant red rock formations. The area is surrounded by open sagebrush flats and scattered juniper, providing a quiet, spacious place to camp. The surrounding landscape invites walking, photography, and wildlife watching. Lone Mesa is an excellent camp base for exploring Canyonlands National Park, Dead Horse Point State Park, and nearby mountain bike or 4WD routes.

The campground has designated sites, each with a picnic table and fire ring. There are no vault toilets or potable water, so campers must be fully self-contained and pack out all waste. Both tents and RVs are welcome. Camping is first-come, first-served.

Photos: https://t2bk.com/SW

70. GOBLIN VALLEY OVERLOOK DISPERSED CAMPING - FREE

- Goblin Valley State Park
- Temple Mt Road
- Green River, UT 84525
- GPS: 38.6453, -110.6478

Maps: https://t2bk.com/SX

Goblin Valley Overlook Dispersed Camping is outside Goblin Valley State Park in Utah. It has a wide-open desert setting with views of the park's otherworldly sandstone formations and surrounding badlands. The area features sandy flats, scattered rock outcrops, and sparse vegetation like sagebrush and juniper. There are no formal trails from the campsites, but the surrounding terrain invites exploration on foot and offers excellent opportunities for photography and stargazing. Wildlife sightings may include lizards, jackrabbits, and a variety of desert birds.

There are no designated sites, vault toilets, or potable water, so you must be self-sufficient, bringing all necessary supplies and packing out all waste. Both tents and RVs are welcome. First-come, first-served. It's a quiet base in this very unique landscape.

Photos: https://t2bk.com/SY

71. HORSESHOE CANYON DISPERSED CAMPING - FREE

- BLM
- Lower San Rafael Rd.
- Hanksville, UT 84734
- GPS: 38.4738, -110.2001

Maps: https://t2bk.com/SZ

Horseshoe Canyon Dispersed Camping is located near the remote Horseshoe Canyon unit of Canyonlands National Park, renowned for its dramatic canyon scenery and some of the finest ancient rock art in the United States. The camping area is on BLM land outside the park boundary in a rugged desert landscape of sandy flats, juniper, sagebrush, and distant sandstone cliffs. Visitors can explore the surrounding open desert or access the trailhead leading into Horseshoe Canyon. Wildlife commonly seen in the area includes lizards, jackrabbits, and a variety of raptors.

Camping is dispersed, with no designated sites, vault toilets, or potable water. Visitors must be fully self-contained and pack out all waste. Tents and RVs are welcome. First-come, first-served.

Photos: https://t2bk.com/TA

72. LEDGE-A CAMPGROUND - $20/$10

- BLM
- Kane Springs Rd.
- Moab, UT 84532
- GPS: 38.4807, -109.6032

Maps: https://t2bk.com/TB

Ledge-A Campground is near Moab, Utah, along the Kane Creek Road corridor, set against the backdrop of striking red rock cliffs and desert mesas. The campground offers a classic high-desert setting with scattered juniper and pinyon pine, providing partial shade and a rugged atmosphere. It's close to popular rock climbing areas, off-road trails, and hiking routes, making it a convenient base for outdoor activities. Wildlife sightings may include lizards, desert cottontails, and a variety of birds.

The campground has designated sites, each with a picnic table and fire ring. Vault toilets are available, but there is no potable water, so campers must bring their own. Tents and small RVs or trailers can be accommodated. Camping is first-come, first-served.

Photos: https://t2bk.com/TC

73. CREEK PASTURE CAMPGROUND - $15/$7.50

- BLM
- Utah 211 Scenic
- La Sal, UT 84530
- GPS: 38.1657, -109.6317

Maps: https://t2bk.com/TE

Creek Pasture Campground is near La Sal, Utah, along the Indian Creek corridor, surrounded by towering sandstone cliffs, open desert, and scattered juniper trees. The campground is near a seasonal creek and offers stunning views of the surrounding red rock landscape. It's a favorite spot for climbers, hikers, and photographers exploring Indian Creek and the Bears Ears region. There are no formal trails from the campground, but the area offers plenty of space for walking and enjoying the scenery. Wildlife sightings may include mule deer, lizards, and a variety of desert birds.

The campground has designated sites, each with a picnic table and fire ring. Vault toilets are available, but there is no potable water. Campsites accommodate tents and small RVs or trailers. First-come, first-served.

Photos: https://t2bk.com/TF

74. PETER'S POINT DISPERSED CAMPING - FREE

- Manti-La Sal National Forest
- FR 1075
- Monticello, UT 84535
- GPS: 37.9559, -109.3804

Maps: https://t2bk.com/TG

Peter's Point Dispersed Camping is located in the Manti-La Sal National Forest near La Sal, Utah, at around 8,500 feet. The area offers a cool mountain setting with sweeping views of the surrounding La Sal Mountains, forested slopes, and distant desert valleys. This is not "red rock and arches" Utah. The landscape is a mix of open meadows, aspen stands, and patches of spruce and fir, creating a peaceful, scenic atmosphere. Nearby forest roads and the surrounding terrain provide opportunities for hiking, wildlife viewing, and photography. Wildlife sightings may include deer, elk, marmots, and a variety of mountain birds.

Camping here is dispersed, with no designated sites, vault toilets, or potable water. Campers must be self-contained and pack out all waste. Tents and RVs are welcome. Camping is first-come, first-served.

Photos: https://t2bk.com/TH

75. THE NEEDLES CAMPGROUND - $20/$10

- Canyonlands National Park
- Utah 211
- Monticello, UT 84535
- GPS: 38.1498, -109.801

Maps: https://t2bk.com/UY

The Needles Campground is in the Needles District of Canyonlands National Park, surrounded by colorful sandstone spires, cliffs, and desert mesas. Set among pinyon pines and junipers, the campground provides shade and stunning views of the red rock landscape. Several trailheads are located nearby, offering access to a network of hiking routes that wind through canyons, past arches, and around towering rock formations. Visitors often spot wildlife such as mule deer, lizards, and a variety of desert birds.

Photos: https://t2bk.com/UZ

The campground offers designated sites, each with a picnic table and fire ring. Vault toilets are available, and drinking water is provided seasonally. Campsites accommodate tents and small RVs or trailers. Some sites can be reserved in advance, and others are first-come, first-served.

4
SOUTHEAST UTAH

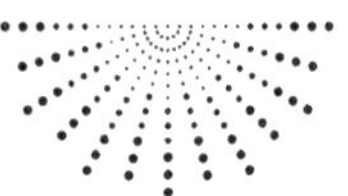

MONUMENT CORNER, BEARS EARS, VALLEY OF THE GODS, HOVENWEEP, RAINBOW BRIDGE

77. GOOSENECKS CAMPGROUND - $10

- Goosenecks State Park
- Hwy 316
- Mexican Hat, UT 84531
- GPS: 37.1746, -109.9271

Maps: https://t2bk.com/TI

Goosenecks Campground is in Goosenecks State Park in southeastern Utah, perched on the rim of a deep canyon carved by the San Juan River. The campground has stunning panoramic views of the famous river meanders that twist through the desert landscape far below. This high-desert setting has scattered juniper, sagebrush, and wide-open skies, making it an excellent spot for photography, stargazing, and quiet reflection. There are no formal hiking trails, but visitors often explore the canyon rim on foot and take in the sweeping vistas.

The campground has designated sites with picnic tables and fire rings. Vault toilets are available, but there is no potable water. Sites are suitable for tents, small RVs, or trailers. All camping is first-come, first-served.

Photos: https://t2bk.com/TJ

78. VALLEY OF THE GODS DISPERSED CAMPING - FREE

- BLM
- Valley of the Gods Rd.
- Mexican Hat, UT 84531
- GPS: 37.3158, -109.851

Maps: https://t2bk.com/TK

Valley of the Gods Dispersed Camping is near Mexican Hat, Utah, in a stunning desert landscape filled with towering sandstone buttes, mesas, and spires. The area offers an iconic red rock backdrop and a peaceful, remote atmosphere perfect for photography, sightseeing, and quiet exploration. There are no formal hiking trails, but visitors can wander the open desert or follow the dirt road network that winds through the valley. Wildlife sightings may include lizards, jackrabbits, and desert birds.

Camping here is dispersed, with no designated sites, vault toilets, or potable water. Campers must be fully self-sufficient and pack out all waste. Tents and RVs are welcome, though the ground is mostly sandy and rocky. First-come, first-served

Photos: https://t2bk.com/TL

79. DEVILS CANYON CAMPGROUND - $20/$10

- Manti-La Sal National Forest
- U.S. 191
- Blanding, UT 84511
- GPS: 37.7367, -109.4114

Maps: https://t2bk.com/TM

Devils Canyon Campground is in the Manti-La Sal National Forest near Monticello, Utah, at about 7,400 feet elevation. The campground is set among towering ponderosa pine, juniper, and oak trees, offering a cool, shaded atmosphere with beautiful views of the surrounding mesas and canyons. Nearby trails and forest roads provide excellent hiking, mountain biking, and wildlife viewing, with deer, turkeys, and various songbirds often spotted in the area.

The campground offers around 40 sites, each with a picnic table, fire ring, and grill. Vault toilets are available, and drinking water is provided seasonally. Sites accommodate tents, trailers, and small to medium RVs. Some sites can be reserved and others are first-come, first-served. The campground typically operates from late spring through early fall.

Photos: https://t2bk.com/TN

80. MULEY POINT DISPERSED CAMPING - FREE

Glen Canyon National Recreation Area
Muley Point Road
Mexican Hat, UT
GPS: 37.2352, -109.9923

Maps: https://t2bk.com/TO

Muley Point Dispersed Camping is located at the edge of Cedar Mesa within Glen Canyon National Recreation Area, offering one of the most breathtaking overlooks in southern Utah. The area provides sweeping views over the deep canyons of the San Juan River, Monument Valley, and distant desert landscapes. The setting mixes slickrock, sandy soil, and sparse desert vegetation, creating a rugged and remote atmosphere. Visitors can explore the mesa rim on foot and enjoy photography, stargazing, and quiet reflection. Wildlife sightings may include lizards, ravens, and desert songbirds.

Look for the camping area on the right, just before the end of the road. Camping is dispersed without designated sites, vault toilets, or potable water. Campers must be fully self-contained and pack out all waste. Tents and RVs are welcome. Camping is first-come, first-served.

Photos: https://t2bk.com/TP

81. NATURAL BRIDGES CAMPGROUND - $16/$8

- Natural Bridges National Monument
- Natural Bridge
- Lake Powell, UT 84533
- GPS: 37.6093, -109.9837

Maps: https://t2bk.com/TQ

Natural Bridges Campground is located within Natural Bridges National Monument in southern Utah, surrounded by pinyon pine, juniper, and stunning desert scenery. Set at about 6,500 feet, the campground offers a peaceful, high-desert setting close to the monument's three iconic stone bridges. Several hiking trails begin nearby, leading visitors through canyons and dramatic viewpoints. The area is excellent for photography, stargazing, and wildlife watching, with common sightings of mule deer, jackrabbits, and various desert birds.

The campground has thirteen designated sites, each with a picnic table and fire ring. Vault toilets are available, but there is no potable water, so campers must bring their own supplies. Sites accommodate tents and small RVs or trailers. All camping is first-come, first-served.

Photos: https://t2bk.com/TR

82. CEDAR MESA CAMPGROUND - FREE

- Capitol Reef National Park
- Notom-Bullfrog Rd.
- Torrey, UT 84775
- GPS: 38.0071, -111.0848

Maps: https://t2bk.com/TS

Cedar Mesa Campground is located in the southern section of Capitol Reef National Park. It is set on a high mesa surrounded by pinyon pine and juniper and offers expansive views of the Waterpocket Fold. The area provides a quiet, remote desert setting perfect for visitors seeking solitude and access to backcountry hiking. Nearby trails lead to canyons, slickrock, and viewpoints across the rugged landscape. Wildlife sightings include mule deer, lizards, and a variety of desert birds.

The campground has five designated primitive sites, each with a picnic table and fire ring. There are no vault toilets or potable water, so campers must be fully self-sufficient and pack out all waste. Sites are suitable for tents and small RVs. First-come, first-served.

Photos: https://t2bk.com/TT

83. COMB WASH CAMPGROUND - FREE

- BLM
- Comb Wash
- Blanding, UT 84511
- GPS: 37.5078, -109.6548

Maps: https://t2bk.com/TU

Comb Wash Campground is near Blanding, Utah, along the base of Comb Ridge, a striking sandstone formation that stretches for miles across the landscape. The campground sits in a cottonwood-shaded area along Comb Wash, offering a peaceful desert setting with views of red rock cliffs and rugged canyons. The surrounding area is popular for hiking, exploring archaeological sites, and off-road driving. Visitors may encounter mule deer, lizards, and a variety of desert birds.

The campground has several primitive, first-come, first-served sites with picnic tables and fire rings. There are vault toilets but no potable water, so bring your own. Sites accommodate tents, small trailers, and RVs.

Photos: https://t2bk.com/TV

84. MULE CANYON DISPERSED CAMPING - FREE

- BLM
- Mule Canyon Trailhead
- Blanding, UT 84511
- GPS: 37.5391, -109.731

Maps: https://t2bk.com/TX

Mule Canyon Dispersed Camping is near Blanding, Utah, along the scenic Comb Ridge and close to the well-known Mule Canyon ruins and hiking trail. The area is a mix of sandy flats, juniper trees, and red rock surroundings, offering a beautiful desert backdrop with easy access to explore nearby archaeological sites and canyon trails. The nearby Mule Canyon trail offers excellent hiking through a beautiful canyon with Ancestral Puebloan ruins. Wildlife like mule deer, lizards, and desert birds are often seen.

Camping here is dispersed without designated sites, vault toilets, or potable water. Campers must be self-sufficient and pack out all waste. Tents and RVs are welcome. First-come, first-served.

Photos: https://t2bk.com/TY

85. SAND ISLAND CAMPGROUND - $15/$7.50

- BLM
- Sand Island Road
- Bluff, UT 84512
- GPS: 37.2612, -109.6173

Maps: https://t2bk.com/TZ

Sand Island Campground is near Bluff, Utah, along the banks of the San Juan River, surrounded by cottonwood trees, sandstone cliffs, and desert scenery. The campground is a popular launch point for river trips and provides easy access to the Sand Island petroglyph panel, where visitors can view centuries-old rock art carved into the cliff face. The area is great for walking along the river and exploring nearby archaeological sites. Wildlife sightings may include waterfowl, lizards, and desert birds.

The campground has designated sites, each with a picnic table and fire ring. Vault toilets are available, and potable water is provided seasonally. Campsites can accommodate tents, trailers, and small RVs. Camping is first-come, first-served.

Photos: https://t2bk.com/UA

86. ELK MOUNTAIN DISPERSED CAMPING - FREE

- BLM
- Elk Mountain Road
- Blanding, UT 84511
- GPS: 37.5981, -109.9176

Maps: https://t2bk.com/UB

Elk Mountain Dispersed Camping is near Bluff, Utah, in a remote high-desert landscape at the base of Elk Ridge, part of the greater Bears Ears region. This area is rugged terrain with scattered pinyon pine and juniper, as well as expansive views of red rock mesas and desert canyons. The surrounding landscape invites exploration on foot and offers excellent photography and wildlife viewing opportunities. Visitors may spot mule deer, elk, lizards, and desert birds.

Camping here is dispersed, with no designated sites, vault toilets, or potable water. Campers must be completely self-sufficient and pack out all waste. Tents and RVs are welcome. Camping is available on a first-come, first-served basis.

Photos: https://t2bk.com/UC

87. STANTON CREEK CAMPGROUND - $12/$6

- Glen Canyon National Recreation Area
- Stanton Creek Road
- Lake Powell, UT 84533
- GPS: 37.5001, -110.6983

Maps: https://t2bk.com/UD

Stanton Creek Campground is on the southwestern shore of Lake Powell within Glen Canyon National Recreation Area, near Bullfrog, Utah. The area is open desert terrain with sandy flats, rocky outcrops, and scattered juniper, providing direct access to the lake's shoreline. Visitors can walk along the water, explore nearby coves, and enjoy fishing, boating, and photography. Wildlife commonly seen includes waterfowl, lizards, and occasionally mule deer.

Camping at Stanton Creek is dispersed and primitive, with no designated campsites or hookups. Vault toilets are seasonally available, but there is no potable water, so bring your own supply. Tents and RVs are welcome. First-come, first-served.

Photos: https://t2bk.com/UE

88. DEER CREEK CAMPGROUND - $10/$5

- Grand Staircase-Escalante National Monument
- Burr Trail
- Boulder, UT 84716
- GPS: 37.8548, -111.3554

Maps: https://t2bk.com/UH

Deer Creek Campground is in Grand Staircase-Escalante National Monument along the Burr Trail near Boulder, Utah. Sitting beside Deer Creek, the campground is surrounded by cottonwood trees, steep sandstone cliffs, and desert scrub, offering shade and striking scenery. The nearby creek provides a peaceful atmosphere and attracts mule deer, songbirds, and lizards. The surrounding canyons and slickrock invite exploration on foot, and the Burr Trail offers excellent scenic driving and photography opportunities.

The campground has seven designated sites, each with a picnic table and fire ring. Vault toilets are available, but there is no potable water, so you must bring your own. Sites accommodate tents and small RVs. Camping is first-come, first-served.

Photos: https://t2bk.com/UI

89. RECAPTURE RESERVOIR DISPERSED CAMPING - FREE

- BLM
- Radio Hill Road
- Blanding, UT 84511
- GPS: 37.6669, -109.4436

Maps: https://t2bk.com/UJ

Recapture Reservoir Dispersed Camping is located near Blanding, Utah, set along the shores of Recapture Reservoir in a quiet, high-desert environment. The area landscape is open terrain with scattered juniper and pinyon pine, with views of the Abajo Mountains and surrounding mesas. The reservoir provides fishing, kayaking, and wildlife watching opportunities, with common sightings of waterfowl, mule deer, and small mammals. There are no formal hiking trails from the camping area, but visitors can explore the shoreline and nearby hills on foot.

Camping is dispersed, first-come, first-served, with no designated sites, vault toilets, or potable water. Campers should be self-sufficient and pack out all waste. Tents and RVs are welcome, though the ground is mostly uneven and rocky.

Photos: https://t2bk.com/UK

90. BIG FLAT DISPERSED CAMPING - FREE

- BLM
- BLM-107
- Escalante, UT 84726
- GPS: 37.7509, -111.5049

Maps: https://t2bk.com/UL

Big Flat Dispersed Camping is located near Escalante, Utah, on public land within the expansive landscapes of Grand Staircase-Escalante National Monument. The area consists of wide, open flats surrounded by juniper and pinyon pine, with views of distant mesas, sandstone formations, and the Kaiparowits Plateau. This quiet, remote area is ideal for solitude, photography, and stargazing. Nearby dirt roads and open terrain allow for hiking and exploration. Wildlife sightings may include mule deer, lizards, and a variety of desert birds.

Camping is dispersed with no designated sites, vault toilets, or potable water. First-come, first-served. Campers must be self-sufficient and pack out all waste. Tents and RVs are welcome.

Photos: https://t2bk.com/UM

91. LITTLE SPENCER FLAT DISPERSED CAMPING - FREE

- Grand Staircase-Escalante National Monument
- Spencer Flat Road
- Escalante, UT 84726
- GPS: 37.7231, -111.4381

Maps: https://t2bk.com/UN

Little Spencer Flat Dispersed Camping is located within Grand Staircase-Escalante National Monument near Escalante, Utah, in a quiet desert setting surrounded by slickrock, juniper, and scattered pinyon pine. The landscape includes expansive sandstone flats and views of colorful cliffs and distant mesas, creating a quiet and scenic backdrop. The open terrain invites exploration on foot, photography, and enjoying the solitude of the desert. Wildlife sightings may include mule deer, lizards, and a variety of desert birds.

Camping is dispersed, with no designated sites, vault toilets, or potable water. Campers should be self-sufficient and pack out all waste. Tents and RVs are welcome, though the ground is mostly sandy and uneven. Camping is on a first-come, first-served basis.

Photos: https://t2bk.com/UO

92. HOVENWEEP CAMPGROUND - $20/$10

- Hovenweep National Monument
- CR-268A
- Montezuma Creek, CO 84534
- GPS: 37.383, -109.0713

Maps: https://t2bk.com/UQ

Hovenweep Campground is located in Hovenweep National Monument near the Utah-Colorado border, set on a high desert mesa surrounded by juniper, sagebrush, and stunning views of the distant Sleeping Ute Mountain. The campground is within walking distance of the monument's ancient stone towers and dwellings, with the Square Tower Loop Trail starting nearby for easy exploration of the archaeological sites and canyon overlooks. The area is peaceful and quiet, offering excellent stargazing and photography opportunities. Wildlife sightings may include mule deer, cottontail rabbits, and a variety of desert birds.

The campground has 31 sites, each with a picnic table and fire ring. Vault toilets are available, but there is no potable water, so campers must bring their own. Sites accommodate tents and small RVs or trailers. Camping is first-come, first-served.

Photos: https://t2bk.com/UR

93. SEVEN SAILORS VIEW DISPERSED CAMPING - FREE

- BLM
- Valley of the Gods Rd.
- Mexican Hat, UT 84531
- GPS: 37.2414, -109.8168

Maps: https://t2bk.com/XZ

Seven Sailors View offers dispersed camping in the Valley of the Gods region near Mexican Hat, Utah. The site overlooks the striking Seven Sailors sandstone formation, which rises from the desert floor against a backdrop of mesas and buttes. The terrain is open and arid, with sandy flats, red rock, and sparse desert vegetation. The area is quiet and remote. Wildlife, including jackrabbits, coyotes, and raptors, is occasionally spotted.

Camping is primitive with no designated sites, toilets, water, or other amenities. Both tents and RVs are permitted. Campers must be fully self-sufficient and follow Leave No Trace practices. A free permit may be required depending on land designation. Camping is available year-round.

Photos: https://t2bk.com/YA

94. FOOT BRIDGE ROAD DISPERSED CAMPING - FREE

- BLM
- Foot Bridge Rd.
- Bluff, UT 84512
- GPS: 37.2844, -109.4946

Maps: https://t2bk.com/UU

Foot Bridge Road Dispersed Camping is just outside Bluff, Utah, tucked along the San Juan River beneath sandstone cliffs and wide desert skies. The area is a mix of sandy flats, scattered juniper, and rocky outcrops, creating a quiet, scenic place to stay. Visitors can wander the riverbanks or nearby canyons, enjoying opportunities for birdwatching, photography, and peaceful walks. The setting feels remote, with little development and expansive views. Wildlife in the area may include mule deer, jackrabbits, and hawks circling overhead.

This is a primitive, dispersed camping area with no marked sites, toilets, or drinking water. Campers need to be self-reliant and pack out all trash. Tents, vans, and smaller RVs can camp here. Sites are first-come, first-served.

Photos: https://t2bk.com/UV

95. CALF CREEK CAMPGROUND - $15/$7.50

- Grand Staircase-Escalante National Monument
- Hwy 12
- Boulder, UT 84716
- GPS: 37.794, -111.4148

Maps: https://t2bk.com/WD

Calf Creek Campground is located within Grand Staircase-Escalante National Monument along Calf Creek beneath tall sandstone cliffs and shaded by cottonwood trees. The campground is a lush oasis in the desert, with a year-round creek that attracts wildlife, including mule deer, songbirds, and lizards. The popular Lower Calf Creek Falls Trail begins nearby, leading hikers on a scenic 6-mile round trip to a stunning 126-foot waterfall. The area is ideal for hiking, birdwatching, photography, and relaxing by the water.

The campground has thirteen designated sites, each with a picnic table and fire ring. Vault toilets and drinking water are available during the main season. Sites can accommodate tents and small RVs or trailers. First-come, first-served.

Photos: https://t2bk.com/WE

96. HARRIS WASH DISPERSED CAMPING - FREE

- Grand Staircase-Escalante National Monument
- Harris Wash Road
- Garfield, UT
- GPS: 37.6045, -111.4231

Maps: https://t2bk.com/UW

Harris Wash Dispersed Camping is located in the Grand Staircase-Escalante National Monument near Escalante, Utah. It offers a quiet, remote setting surrounded by slickrock, sandy flats, and scattered juniper. The area provides sweeping views of surrounding cliffs and mesas and easy access to explore the wash. Hikers can follow the wash downstream, enjoying sculpted sandstone walls, natural pools, and hidden side canyons. Wildlife sightings may include mule deer, lizards, and desert birds.

Camping here is undeveloped, with no designated sites, toilets, or drinking water. Campers must be fully prepared to pack in supplies and pack out all waste. Tents and RVs are welcome, though the ground is uneven. First-come, first-served.

Photos: https://t2bk.com/UX

97. JACOB'S CHAIR TRAILHEAD DISPERSED CAMPING - FREE

- BLM
- Utah 95
- Fry Canyon, UT 84533
- GPS: 37.7069, -110.2392

Maps: https://t2bk.com/VA

Jacob's Chair Trailhead Dispersed Camping is located near Fry Canyon, Utah. It's in a quiet desert setting beneath the towering sandstone called Jacob's Chair. The area is surrounded by open sagebrush flats, scattered juniper, and expansive views of nearby cliffs and mesas. The trail leading to Jacob's Chair begins nearby, providing an adventurous hike to the base of the landmark with panoramic views along the way. Wildlife sightings may include mule deer, lizards, and desert birds.

Camping is dispersed with no designated sites, vault toilets, or drinking water. Campers must be self-sufficient and pack out all trash and waste. Tents and RVs can be accommodated on the mostly flat, sandy terrain. Camping is available on a first-come, first-served basis.

Photos: https://t2bk.com/VB

98. STARR SPRINGS CAMPGROUND - $10/$5

- BLM
- Starr Springs Campground Rd.
- Ticaboo, UT
- GPS: 37.8491, -110.6633

Maps: https://t2bk.com/VE

Starr Springs Campground is located near the base of Mount Hillers in southern Utah, offering quiet camping beneath large cottonwood and juniper trees. Surrounded by red rock cliffs and desert scenery, the campground provides shade and a peaceful atmosphere in a remote setting. A natural spring flows nearby, creating a small oasis that attracts wildlife such as mule deer, songbirds, and small mammals. The area is popular for hiking, photography, and exploring nearby backroads that lead deeper into the Henry Mountains.

The campground includes twelve designated sites, each with a picnic table and fire ring. Vault toilets are available, but there is no potable water, so you should bring your own supply. The sites accommodate tents and small RVs. Camping is first-come, first-served

Photos: https://t2bk.com/VF

99. HENRY MOUNTAINS VIEW DISPERSED CAMPING - FREE

- BLM
- Starr Springs Campground Rd.
- Lake Powell, UT 84533
- GPS: 37.8246, -110.6425

Maps: https://t2bk.com/VC

Henry Mountains View Dispersed Camping is near Lake Powell, Utah, offering sweeping vistas of the Henry Mountains rising above the desert landscape. The landscape is open flats with scattered juniper and sagebrush, providing a quiet and remote setting with wide, unobstructed views of mesas, canyons, and distant cliffs. The surrounding terrain is excellent for exploration on foot, and nearby dirt roads lead to additional scenic overlooks and backcountry routes. Wildlife sightings may include mule deer, pronghorn, and a variety of desert birds.

Camping here is dispersed with no designated sites, vault toilets, or drinking water. Campers should be self-sufficient and pack out all waste. Tents and RVs are welcome, with plenty of space to spread out on the open ground. First-come, first-served.

Photos: https://t2bk.com/VD

100. BLUE MOUNTAIN DISPERSED CAMPING - FREE

- Manti-La Sal National Forest
- Forest Road 0086
- Monticello, UT 84535
- GPS: 37.8623, -109.4333

Maps: https://t2bk.com/VX

Blue Mountain Dispersed Camping is in the Manti-La Sal National Forest near Monticello, Utah. It offers cool, high-elevation camping surrounded by aspen, pine, and spruce trees. The area has beautiful views of the Abajo Mountains and distant desert mesas, with a peaceful forest setting ideal for relaxing or exploring. Nearby forest roads and paths provide access to hiking, mountain biking, and wildlife viewing. Visitors may encounter deer, wild turkeys, and a variety of mountain birds.

Camping here is dispersed, with no designated sites, vault toilets, or drinking water. Campers must be self-reliant and pack out all trash and waste. Tents and RVs are welcome, and several clearings and level areas are suitable for setting up camp. Camping is first-come, first-served.

Photos: https://t2bk.com/VY

101. WINDWHISTLE CAMPGROUND - $20/$10

- BLM
- Needles Overlook Road
- Monticello, UT 84535
- GPS: 38.1774, -109.4621

Maps: https://t2bk.com/VZ

Windwhistle Campground is located in the Canyon Rims Recreation Area near Monticello, Utah, tucked against the sandstone walls of Roan Bailey Mesa at approximately 6,000 feet. The campground offers a peaceful desert setting with pinyon-juniper woodlands and views of the La Sal and Abajo Mountains. A half-mile nature trail begins near the group site, winding through native vegetation and offering interpretive signs. The area is ideal for hiking, photography, and stargazing under dark skies. Nearby attractions include Needles Overlook and Indian Creek.

Photos: https://t2bk.com/WA

The campground features 15 individual sites and one reservable group site. Each site includes a picnic table, fire ring, and grill. Vault toilets and trash receptacles are available. Drinking water is provided seasonally from May through October. Sites accommodate tents and small to medium RVs, with some pull-through options. All individual sites are first-come, first-served.

102. HATCH POINT CAMPGROUND - $20/$10

- BLM
- Hatch Point Rd.
- Monticello, UT 84535
- GPS: 38.3807, -109.6169

Maps: https://t2bk.com/WB

Hatch Point Campground is in the Canyon Rims Recreation Area near Monticello, Utah, perched atop a high desert mesa at approximately 5,774 feet elevation. The campground offers sweeping views of red rock canyons, mesas, and distant mountain ranges, providing a quiet and remote setting ideal for stargazing and photography. Nearby attractions include Anticline Overlook and Kane Creek Anticline, offering dramatic canyon vistas. The area is also a gateway to hiking, biking, and off-road trails throughout the Canyon Rims region.

The campground has 10 sites, each with a picnic table, fire ring, and grill. Vault toilets and trash receptacles are available, but there is no potable water, so you should bring your own supply. Sites accommodate tents and small to medium RVs, with some pull-through options. Camping is first-come, first-served.

Photos: https://t2bk.com/WC

5

SOUTHWEST UTAH

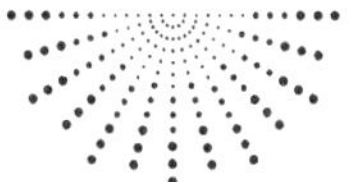

REDROCKS, ZION, BRYCE, GRAND STAIRCASE-ESCALANTE, CAPITOL REEF, CEDAR BREAKS

104. TOM'S BEST SPRING DISPERSED CAMPING - FREE

- Dixie National Forest
- Tom's Best Spring Rd. (FR-117)
- Panguitch, UT 84759
- GPS: 37.728, -112.2487

Maps: https://t2bk.com/WF

Tom's Best Spring Dispersed Camping is near Bryce Canyon National Park. It's a quiet, forested setting among ponderosa pines and open clearings. The area has a wide range of dispersed sites along Forest Road 117, with plenty of space for tents, trailers, and RVs. Many sites are shaded and spread out, giving campers privacy and easy access to nature. The surrounding forest is ideal for walking, wildlife viewing, and relaxing.

Photos: https://t2bk.com/WG

Outdoor activities nearby include hiking and mountain biking on trails in Red Canyon and the Paunsaugunt Plateau. The landscape features forested ridges, meadows, and rocky outcrops, offering panoramic views across the surrounding terrain. There are no designated campsites or facilities, so campers must be fully self-sufficient and pack out all trash. Camping is first-come, first-served.

105. NORTH CREEK DISPERSED CAMPING - FREE

- BLM
- Kolob Terrace Rd.
- Virgin, UT 84779
- GPS: 37.2203, -113.1616

Maps: https://t2bk.com/WJ

North Creek Dispersed Camping is located near Virgin, Utah, along Kolob Terrace Road, approximately 20 minutes from the west entrance of Zion National Park. This area offers a variety of informal campsites among cottonwood trees and near the creek, providing a peaceful setting with natural shade and the soothing sound of flowing water. The landscape features red rock formations, open skies, and a mix of desert and riparian environments, making it ideal for photography, stargazing, and relaxation.

Visitors can enjoy hiking, viewing wildlife, and exploring trails that lead into the surrounding wilderness. There are no designated campsites or amenities, and the area is suitable for tents, vans, and small RVs. Access to some sites may require high-clearance vehicles, especially after rain. Camping is on a first-come, first-served basis.

Photos: https://t2bk.com/WK

106. CAPITOL REEF OVERFLOW DISPERSED CAMPING - FREE

- Fishlake National Forest
- Hwy 24
- Torrey, UT 84775
- GPS: 38.3267, -111.3641

Maps: https://t2bk.com/WL

Capitol Reef Overflow Dispersed Camping is located in Fishlake National Forest near Torrey, Utah, just outside the west entrance of Capitol Reef National Park. This high-desert landscape features open spaces with scattered pinyon pines and junipers, offering wide views of red rock cliffs and distant mesas. The setting is quiet and informal, with plenty of room to spread out along the forest roads. It's a popular choice for those visiting Capitol Reef who prefer a more rustic experience.

Campers often use the area as a base for hiking, photography, and stargazing. There are no designated sites, facilities, or water sources, so campers must be self-reliant and pack out all waste. Tents and RVs are welcome, and the terrain is generally flat and accessible. First-come, first-served.

Photos: https://t2bk.com/WM

107. OLD HIGHWAY 89 DISPERSED CAMPING - FREE

- BLM
- Hwy 89
- Mount Carmel, UT 85207
- GPS: 37.2057, -112.675

Maps: https://t2bk.com/WP

Old Highway 89 Dispersed Camping is just off U.S. Route 89 near Mount Carmel Junction, Utah. It's a convenient base for exploring Zion National Park, Coral Pink Sand Dunes, and other nearby attractions. The landscape is open gravel flats and elevated ridges, providing expansive views of the surrounding red rock landscape. Sites are informal and spread out, accommodating tents, vans, and RVs of various sizes.

It's a scenic setting with easy access, with some sites offering fire rings and natural shade. Although there may be some road noise, many find the location peaceful, especially at night. There are no amenities, so visitors should come prepared with their own water and supplies. First-come, first-served.

Photos: https://t2bk.com/WQ

108. HURRICANE CLIFFS DESIGNATED DISPERSED CAMPSITES 36-48 - FREE

- Hurricane Cliffs Recreation Area
- Sheep Bridge Rd.
- La Verkin, UT 84745
- GPS: 37.1866, -113.2228

Maps: https://t2bk.com/WT

Hurricane Cliffs Designated Dispersed Campsites 36–48 are located near Virgin, Utah, on a mesa overlooking wide desert flats and distant red rock formations. The area is mostly open with scattered shrubs and juniper, offering broad views and colorful sunsets. The Hurricane Cliffs Trail System runs nearby, providing access to non-motorized hiking, mountain biking, and horseback riding routes. Wildlife in the area includes jackrabbits, lizards, and raptors, especially active during early morning and evening hours.

There are 13 marked sites in this section, each with a metal fire ring. The sites are spaced apart and suitable for tents, vans, and RVs. There are no restrooms or drinking water available. All camping is first-come, first-served. The area is open year-round.

Photos: https://t2bk.com/WU

109. PYRAMID RIDGE CAMPGROUND - $12/$6

- BLM
- Shurts Left Hand
- Cedar City, UT 84720
- GPS: 37.613, -113.1005

Maps: https://t2bk.com/WV

Pyramid Ridge Campground is just south of Cedar City, Utah, set among pinyon-juniper woodlands at the base of the Hurricane Cliffs. The landscape includes scattered red rock formations and distant views of the surrounding mountains and desert. The campground is next to the Iron Hills Trail System, offering direct access to nearly 30 miles of singletrack trails used for mountain biking, hiking, and running. Wildlife, including mule deer, jackrabbits, and a variety of birds, is often seen in the area.

The campground includes 14 sites, including one group site. Each site has a picnic table, fire ring, and tent pad. Vault toilets and trash bins are available, but there is no drinking water. Campsites accommodate tents, trailers, and RVs up to 50 feet. All sites are reservable online or at the campground using posted QR codes.

Photos: https://t2bk.com/WW

110. BAKER DAM CAMPGROUND - $12/$6

- BLM
- North Baker Lake Rd.
- Veyo, UT 84782
- GPS: 37.3777, -113.6431

Maps: https://t2bk.com/WX

Baker Dam Campground is located near a small reservoir in southwestern Utah, surrounded by juniper and pinyon pine at about 5,000 feet elevation. The red soil and scattered volcanic rock give way to views of the Pine Valley Mountains to the north. A short trail loops near the shoreline, offering chances to view waterfowl like herons and gray flycatchers. The surrounding area supports a variety of wildlife, including deer, quail, and rabbits, with hunting permitted outside the recreation boundary. The reservoir is stocked with rainbow and brown trout.

The campground has 19 single sites and 2 group sites, each with a picnic table and fire ring. Vault toilets and trash bins are provided; however, potable water is not available. Reservations are required for all sites and must be made in advance. The campground is open year-round, although services may be limited during the winter months.

Photos: https://t2bk.com/WY

111. PINE LAKE CAMPGROUND - $26/$13

- Dixie National Forest
- Pine Lake Campground Rd.
- Bryce, UT 84764
- GPS: 37.7456, -111.9525

Maps: https://t2bk.com/WZ

Pine Lake Campground sits at 7,500 feet near the shore of a small alpine lake, surrounded by ponderosa pine and open meadows. Red rock formations and forested hills typical of the Paunsaugunt Plateau characterize the landscape. The Pine Lake Trail offers a short loop with scenic views and connects to longer routes leading into nearby canyons. Wildlife in the area includes mule deer, wild turkeys, and occasional sightings of golden eagles. The lake itself is stocked with trout and sees light fishing activity.

There are 32 campsites, each with a picnic table and fire ring. Vault toilets and drinking water are available. The campground is usually open from late May through early October. Sites can be reserved in advance, though some are available on a first-come, first-served basis. The campground accommodates both tents and small to mid-size RVs.

Photos: https://t2bk.com/XA

112. HOLE-IN-THE-ROCK DISPERSED CAMPING - FREE

- BLM
- Hole in the Rock Road (BLM-200)
- Escalante, UT 84726
- GPS: 37.723, -111.527

Maps: https://t2bk.com/XB

Hole in the Rock Road offers dispersed camping opportunities amid Utah's high desert landscape, characterized by open sagebrush flats, scattered juniper, and sandstone formations. The area provides access to several notable hikes, including Zebra Slot Canyon, Devil's Garden, and Dry Fork Narrows. Wildlife sightings may include mule deer, lizards, and a variety of bird species. The region is also renowned for its dark skies, making it an ideal location for stargazing.

Photos: https://t2bk.com/XC

Camping along Hole-in-the-Rock Road is primitive, with no designated sites or amenities. Campers must bring all necessary supplies, including water, and practice Leave No Trace principles. A free permit is required for overnight stays within the Grand Staircase-Escalante National Monument and can be obtained at local visitor centers. The area is accessible year-round, though conditions may vary.

113. JOHNS VALLEY DISPERSED CAMPING - FREE

- BLM
- Johns Valley Rd.
- Panguitch, UT 84759
- GPS: 37.7316, -112.0945

Maps: https://t2bk.com/XD

Johns Valley dispersed camping is approximately 8 miles northeast of Bryce Canyon National Park. It sits in open meadows and scattered cedar stands along a lightly traveled stretch of Johns Valley Road. The terrain is mostly flat with a mix of sagebrush and juniper, providing partial shade and open sky suitable for solar setups. Mule deer frequent the area, and coyotes are often heard at night. Nearby attractions include Bryce Canyon and Kodachrome Basin State Park.

Camping here is primitive, with no designated sites or amenities. Some areas have existing fire rings, but there are no toilets, water, or trash services. Campers should bring all necessary supplies and follow Leave No Trace principles. Camping is permitted within 150 feet of designated roads and at least 300 feet from water sources. The area is accessible year-round, though conditions may vary.

Photos: https://t2bk.com/XE

114. WHITE HOUSE TRAILHEAD & CAMPGROUND - $12/$6

- Grand Staircase-Escalante National Monument
- White House Trailhead Road
- Kanab, UT 84741
- GPS: 37.08, -111.8904

Maps: https://t2bk.com/XF

White House Campground is next to the Paria River. The terrain features open flats with sparse juniper and sage-brush, offering expansive views of the surrounding cliffs. The campground serves as the primary access point to the Paria Canyon-Vermilion Cliffs Wilderness, including the Paria River Canyon and Buckskin Gulch. Wildlife sightings may include lizards, songbirds, and occasional mule deer.

The campground has seven drive-in and five walk-in sites, each with a picnic table and fire ring. Vault toilets are available, but there is no potable water. All sites are first-come, first-served. The campground is open year-round, although services may be limited during the winter months. A free permit is required for overnight stays in the adjacent Paria Canyon-Vermilion Cliffs Wilderness and can be obtained at nearby visitor centers.

Photos: https://t2bk.com/XG

115. CASTLE ROCK CAMPGROUND - $20

- Fremont Indian State Park
- FR-478
- Sevier, UT 84766
- GPS: 38.5564, -112.3555

Maps: https://t2bk.com/XH

Castle Rock Campground is in Clear Creek Canyon, surrounded by rugged cliffs, pinyon pine, juniper, and cottonwood. The canyon setting offers shade and shelter, as well as access to nearby cultural sites. Short trails connect directly to petroglyph panels and exhibits within Fremont Indian State Park. The creek flows seasonally through the area, attracting birds, small mammals, and mule deer. The natural rock formations give the campground its name and create a scenic backdrop for hiking and photography.

There are 31 campsites suitable for tents and RVs up to 40 feet in length. Each site has a picnic table and fire ring. Facilities include vault toilets, flush restrooms, and potable water. The campground is open seasonally from mid-April to late October. Some sites are reservable, and others are available on a first-come, first-served basis.

Photos: https://t2bk.com/XI

116. PARIA ROAD DISPERSED CAMPING - FREE

- Grand Staircase-Escalante National Monument
- Paria Rd.
- Kanab, UT 84741
- GPS: 37.1976, -111.9823

Maps: https://t2bk.com/XJ

Paria Road offers dispersed camping within Grand Staircase-Escalante National Monument, set among open desert terrain with views of sandstone cliffs and mesas. The area features a mix of sagebrush flats and juniper stands, providing minimal shade but expansive vistas. Nearby attractions include the Paria ghost town site and access to the Paria River. Wildlife sightings include lizards, jackrabbits, and a variety of bird species. The region is renowned for its quiet atmosphere and crystal-clear night skies, making it an ideal destination for stargazing.

Camping along Paria Road is primitive, with no designated sites or amenities. Campers are required to bring all necessary supplies and adhere to Leave No Trace principles. A free permit is required for overnight stays within the Grand Staircase-Escalante National Monument and can be obtained at local visitor centers. The area is accessible year-round, though conditions may vary.

Photos: https://t2bk.com/XK

117. PONDEROSA GROVE CAMPGROUND - $12/$6

- BLM
- Hancock Rd.
- Kanab, UT 84741
- GPS: 37.0889, -112.6723

Maps: https://t2bk.com/XL

Ponderosa Grove Campground is at 6,300 feet in a stand of mature ponderosa pines, surrounded by open sagebrush country and views of the Vermilion Cliffs. Located near the Coral Pink Sand Dunes, the area offers access to off-highway vehicle routes, short hiking trails, and wildlife viewing. Mule deer, jackrabbits, quail, and a variety of raptors are commonly seen. The landscape features red sand, scattered sandstone outcrops, and wide-open skies, making it a good spot for photography and stargazing.

The campground has 35 sites, including options for tents, small RVs, and walk-in camping. Each site has a picnic table and fire ring. Vault toilets and trash collection are available. There is no potable water or hookups. The group site is reservable, but individual sites are available on a first-come, first-served basis. Open year-round, services may be reduced in winter months.

Photos: https://t2bk.com/XM

118. ANDERSON MEADOW CAMPGROUND - $20/$10

- Fishlake National Forest
- FR-574
- Beaver, UT 84713
- GPS: 38.2096, -112.4316

Maps: https://t2bk.com/XN

Anderson Meadow Campground is at about 9,400 feet, tucked in a dense forest of spruce, fir, and aspen above a small reservoir. The setting is quiet and shaded, with clear mountain air and views of surrounding ridgelines. Anderson Meadow Reservoir is popular for fishing for brook and rainbow trout, and wildlife sightings may include elk, deer, marmots, and a variety of songbirds. Hiking opportunities are nearby, and the larger Paiute ATV trail system can be accessed by vehicle from outside the campground.

There are 8 single sites and 2 group sites, each with a picnic table, fire ring, and prep surface. Sites are back-in and suitable for trailers up to 40 feet. Vault toilets and drinking water are available. The campground opens mid-June and typically closes by mid-September.

Photos: https://t2bk.com/XO

119. OVERLOOK POINT DISPERSED CAMPING - FREE

- BLM
- Hwy 24
- Torrey, UT 84775
- GPS: 38.298, -111.3889

Maps: https://t2bk.com/XP

Overlook Point offers dispersed camping just west of Torrey, Utah, with wide views of Capitol Reef's cliffs and canyons. The landscape is characterized by high desert terrain, with scattered juniper, sandy soil, and rocky outcrops. Open skies make this a favorite for stargazing and photography. Sunrise and sunset light up the red rock to the east, and occasional mule deer, jackrabbits, and raptors pass through the area. No formal trails lead from camp, but nearby public lands offer space to explore on foot or by vehicle.

Camping here is primitive with no services or designated sites. Campers must pack in water, supplies, and follow Leave No Trace practices. The area can accommodate both tents and RVs. Camping is allowed year-round. A free permit may be required depending on land designation; check with local BLM offices before setting up.

Photos: https://t2bk.com/XQ

120. KITCHEN CORRAL WASH DISPERSED CAMPING - FREE

- Grand Staircase-Escalante National Monument
- BLM-508
- Kanab, UT 84741
- GPS: 37.1403, -112.0915

Maps: https://t2bk.com/XR

Kitchen Corral Wash offers dispersed camping within Grand Staircase-Escalante National Monument, set in a high desert landscape of red dirt flats, scattered juniper, and low sandstone ridges. You'll find wide-open views and easy access to Buckskin Gulch and the Paria River corridor. Wildlife sightings may include jackrabbits, coyotes, and various birds of prey. The remote location and minimal light pollution make it an ideal spot for stargazing.

Photos: https://t2bk.com/XS

Camping here is primitive, with no designated sites or facilities. Campers are required to bring all necessary supplies and adhere to Leave No Trace principles. The area accommodates tents and RVs, with some spots suitable for larger rigs. A free permit is required for overnight stays within the monument and can be obtained at local visitor centers. The area is accessible year-round, though conditions may vary.

121. RED CLIFFS CAMPGROUND - $15/$7.50

- Red Cliffs National Conservation Area
- Hurricane, UT 84737
- GPS: 37.2225, -113.4034

Maps: https://t2bk.com/XT

Red Cliffs Campground is tucked beneath towering Navajo sandstone cliffs in a desert oasis where Quail Creek flows through cottonwood-lined banks. The area is rich in natural and cultural history, with nearby trails leading to dinosaur tracks, Ancestral Puebloan sites, and pioneer-era structures. The Red Reef Trail follows the creek into a narrow canyon with seasonal pools and waterfalls. The Anasazi Trail offers views of archaeological sites. Wildlife such as Gambel's quail, canyon wrens, and desert tortoises may be observed.

The campground has 11 sites, each with a shade shelter, picnic table, fire ring, and grill. Vault toilets and potable water are available. Sites 6, 7, and 10 offer pull-through parking, and sites 8 and 11 are ADA accessible. Reservations are required for all campsites; walk-ins are not permitted. The campground is open year-round, although services may be limited during the winter months.

Photos: https://t2bk.com/XU

122. GOOSEBERRY MESA DISPERSED CAMPING - FREE

- BLM
- Main Street
- Apple Valley, UT 84737
- GPS: 37.1417, -113.1551

Maps: https://t2bk.com/XV

Gooseberry Mesa offers dispersed camping on a high desert plateau near Apple Valley, Utah, with panoramic views of Zion National Park and surrounding canyons. The terrain includes slickrock, sand, and scattered juniper, creating a rugged setting ideal for photography, hiking, and solitude. The mesa is best known for its network of mountain biking trails, especially the Gooseberry Mesa National Recreation Trail, which crosses exposed rock and winding ridgelines. Wildlife such as jackrabbits, coyotes, and hawks are commonly seen.

Camping is primitive with no designated sites, water, or toilets. Visitors are required to bring all essentials and adhere to Leave No Trace practices. Tents and RVs are accommodated, although high-clearance vehicles are recommended. Camping is allowed year-round.

Photos: https://t2bk.com/XW

123. LEEDS CANYON DESIGNATED DISPERSED CAMPING - FREE

- Dixie National Forest
- FR-032
- Hurricane, UT 84737
- GPS: 37.2667, -113.3702

Maps: https://t2bk.com/XX

Leeds Canyon Designated Dispersed Camping is in a forested section of Dixie National Forest near Leeds, Utah. The area is at the base of the Pine Valley Mountains and features a mix of pinyon, juniper, and oak with patches of red rock and sandy soil. Several of the designated sites are tucked along Leeds Creek, offering some shade and seclusion. Wildlife commonly seen includes mule deer, jackrabbits, and a variety of songbirds and raptors. This spot is popular for its quiet setting, open skies, and access to nearby trails and backroads.

Camping is only allowed in designated, numbered sites—about 13 in total. There are no services such as toilets, trash collection, or water, so campers must bring all supplies and pack out waste. Sites are suitable for tents and smaller RVs. Camping is allowed year-round; no reservations are needed.

Photos: https://t2bk.com/XY

6

CALIFORNIA SIERRA NEVADA MOUNTAINS

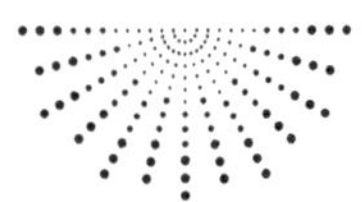

••• TAHOE & SURROUNDING AREA •••

125. LAKES BASIN RECREATION AREA

- Near Graeagle, California
- GPS: 39.7016874,-120.6769558

Map: https://t2bk.com/AAM

Nine miles southwest of Graeagle, California, Lakes Basin is one of Northern California's most beautiful and dramatic areas. Nearby, you will find stunning scenery and over 20 small lakes, most of which you can reach via hiking trails. You'll find a variety of recreational activities, such as camping, fishing, boating, hunting, biking, horseback riding, picnicking, hiking, swimming, windsurfing, and nature study. In the winter, visitors can snowmobile, cross-country ski, and snowshoe.

Lakes Basin Recreation Area includes Gold Lake Campground, Lakes Basin Campground, Packsaddle Campground, Sardine Lake Campground, Goose Lake Campground, Snag Lake Campground, and more.

Photos: https://t2bk.com/AAL

126. GOLD LAKE CAMPGROUND - $22/$11

- Lakes Basin Recreation Area
- Plumas National Forest
- Gold Lake Road
- Graeagle, CA
- GPS: 39.6786, -120.6462

Map: https://t2bk.com/AAN

Gold Lake Campground is located along the shores of Gold Lake at an elevation of 6,400 feet. Eleven of the 37 campsites are available for reservation. The road north of the boat launch facility is narrow and rough, better suited to smaller vehicles and tent campers. The campground is great for boating and fishing.

Photos: https://t2bk.com/AAO

The campsites here are rugged but nice, with many sites near the lake. It's a gorgeous and tranquil area. The lake offers an excellent spot for swimming, and if you're up for a short drive, the Long Lake Trail and Round Lake Trail, both excellent hiking trails, are just 10 minutes away. This spot is part of the Lakes Basin Recreation Area, which includes several other campgrounds, including Packsaddle, Sardine Lake, Goose Lake, and Snag Lake.

127. ALPINE MEADOW CAMPGROUND - $20/$10

- Army Corps of Engineers
- Martis Dam Rd
- Truckee, CA
- GPS: 39.3206, -120.1224

Map: https://t2bk.com/AAR

Martis Creek Lake has a nice campground off the usual path close to Lake Tahoe, Truckee, and Reno. The area around Martis Creek is perfect for those who love hiking, biking, canoeing, kayaking, and trout fishing. The campground is clean and easy to get to, making it a great middle-ground location that offers quick trips to Truckee or Lake Tahoe.

Photos: https://t2bk.com/AAS

Potable water is available in several spots, along with paved pads and bear-proof dumpsters. This is a good choice if you're looking for a camping spot close to Tahoe but with fewer crowds. A small private plane airport is nearby, so there can sometimes be some noise. The facilities are basic, offering some shade and usually a quiet atmosphere. While weekends tend to be busy, it's rare for the campground to be full.

128. INDIAN VALLEY CAMPGROUND - $24/$12

- Tahoe National Forest
- Indian Valley Road
- Camptonville, CA
- GPS: 39.513, -120.981

Maps: https://t2bk.com/AAT

Indian Valley Campground is about 15 miles north of Camptonville. It is on the north bank of the North Yuba River along Highway 49. The campground is paved and has clean, well-maintained, large sites. The sites are spaced out to ensure privacy, and there are options for sun lovers and shade seekers. It has 19 campsites, vault toilets, and piped water. There are no hookups available.

Lying among oak, fir, pine, and madrone trees, the campground has access to the North Yuba Trail and is just 9 miles from Downieville. Facilities include clean pit toilets, fire pits, and picnic tables. Easy river access. It's a popular spot, so it can get quite busy during peak times. A bridge to access the other side of the river is just down the road at Rocky Rest Campground.

Maps: https://t2bk.com/AAU

129. PACKSADDLE CAMPGROUND - $24/$12

- Tahoe National Forest
- Packer Lake Road
- Sierra City, CA 96125
- GPS: 39.6238, -120.6499

Map: https://t2bk.com/AAV

Packsaddle Campground is located among pine and fir trees, with stunning views of the Sierra Buttes and nearby alpine lakes. With 14 well-developed sites, the campground has piped water and vault toilets. It is surrounded by open meadows dotted with wildflowers, overlooking a ravine set against a backdrop of granite mountains. The area is rich with granitic ridges and glacially shaped rock formations, making for breathtaking scenery.

This campground is suitable for tents, RVs, horses, dogs, and kids. It has a clean outhouse, a hand-operated potable water pump, tables, food lockers, dumpsters, and horse corrals. It's perfect for those who love hiking, biking, horseback riding, boating, and fishing in the surrounding lakes. The elevation is 6,000 feet, so expect cooler temperatures.

Photos: https://t2bk.com/AAW

130. WILD PLUM CAMPGROUND - $24/$12

- Tahoe National Forest
- Wild Plum Road
- Sierra City, CA
- GPS: 39.566, -120.601

Map: https://t2bk.com/AAX

Wild Plum Campground is just a mile east of Sierra City along Haypress Creek off Wild Plum Road. It has 47 campsites, piped water, and vault toilets. The campground is close to the Kentucky Mine and Sierra County Historical Park. It's right by the river and has clean facilities, fantastic hiking trails, and views. Several refreshingly cold swimming holes are within walking distance, and a short hike leads to a beautiful waterfall.

Most of the sites at Wild Plum Campground are under a canopy of trees, with dappled sunlight throughout the day. There's a 3-mile loop trail starting right from the campground. This trail winds through the forest, past a waterfall, and along the Pacific Crest Trail (PCT). If you need anything during your stay, Sierra City is nearby, with a small grocery store and a few restaurants.

Photos: https://t2bk.com/AAY

131. LINDSEY LAKE CAMPGROUND - $15

- PG&E
- FSR 17
- Nevada City, CA
- GPS: 39.413, -120.643

Map: https://t2bk.com/ABB

Lindsey Lake Campground has 12 primitive sites with vault toilets and no trash service, so pack it in/pack it out. The only water available is from the lake, so bring your own. Best for tents, vans, or small cab-over-campers only. No big rigs! It is located bout 12 miles north of Highway 20. Good hiking, fishing, and swimming. There's an informal boat launch, and each campsite has a bench, a fire pit, and a bear box. No reservations. First come, first serve.

The road to get there is a bit rocky, so a high-clearance vehicle is recommended. Once you're there, you can enjoy some excellent day hikes and peaceful fishing. Non-motorized boating only. Lake Lindsey is an ideal trailhead for some truly stunning short backpacking trips in the High Sierra.

Photos: https://t2bk.com/ABC

132. COTTONWOOD CREEK CAMPGROUND - $20/$10

- Tahoe National Forest
- Verdi Grade Road
- Sierraville, CA
- GPS: 39.549, -120.317

Map: https://t2bk.com/ABD

Cottonwood Creek Campground is on Highway 89, alongside the seasonal Cottonwood Creek. It's four miles south of Sierraville and an excellent base for outdoor activities like fishing, hunting, hiking, and biking. The campground is tucked away from the highway, offering a peaceful retreat amidst Jeffrey pine and red and white fir trees. The forest canopy provides shade and privacy between sites.

This campground has clean pit toilets, picnic tables, and spacious sites. The Cottonwood Creek Botanical Trail and Overlook Trail start right within the campground. Sites range from small for tents only to larger for big rigs. If you need supplies or a meal out, Sierraville is close by and has a small gas station/market and restaurants.

Photos: https://t2bk.com/ABE

••• YOSEMITE AREA •••

133. BEARDSLEY DAM CAMPGROUND - $25/$12.50

- Stanislaus National Forest
- Forest Route 5N02
- Tuolumne, CA
- GPS: 38.21, -120.075

Map: https://t2bk.com/ABF

Beardsley Dam Campground is a peaceful and scenic camping area near Beardsley Dam along Forest Road 5N02 at the southern end of Beardsley Reservoir. Each campsite has a picnic table, a metal fire ring, and bear-proof lockers. The campground has potable water, vault toilets, and trash service. The campground is first-come, first-served.

Photos: https://t2bk.com/ABG

With twenty-six individual sites and additional group sites, it's an excellent spot for those seeking a quiet and relaxing escape. Campers will enjoy stunning views of the lake. The campground can accommodate RVs and trailers up to a maximum length of 36 feet, making it suitable for various campers. The beautiful lake offers excellent beach spots and good hiking and fishing.

134. FRASER FLAT CAMPGROUND $25/$12.50

- Stanislaus National Forest
- Forest Route 4N42
- Long Barn, CA 95335
- GPS: 38.17, -120.07

Map: https://t2bk.com/ABH

Frasier Flat Campground is in the Stanislaus National Forest and is super tidy and well-kept. The pit toilets are always clean. The campsites are all flat, and there are a couple of double sites. There are both sunny and shady sites. The south fork of the Stanislaus River runs right alongside the campground, making it perfect for some quality fishing.

The campground has a nice hike that follows the river and offers inspiring granite views. The nearby Strawberry Grade trail used to be an old mining railroad, but now it's a nice path for a walk or a bike ride. It's a good place for hanging out, fishing, hiking, or kicking back and enjoying the Sierra's beauty. However, it can get busy on the weekends!

Photos: https://t2bk.com/ABI

135. HARDIN FLAT ROAD DISPERSED CAMPSITES - FREE

- Stanislaus National Forest
- Hardin Flat Rd
- Groveland, CA
- GPS: 37.8111, -119.9056

Map: https://t2bk.com/ABJ

Dispersed camping. This is not a campground. This campsite is conveniently located just 3 miles from Yosemite's entrance, making it an excellent choice for those wanting to explore the park. Thanks to its clear, open skies, it's excellent if you're using solar. The road to the campsite branches off from the main road and stretches along for a way, so feel free to drive along and pick out your ideal spot. Along Hardin Flat Road, you'll find various camping options, some offering open views while others are in the bush for more privacy.

And here's a quirky detail – if you hear bells during the night, there's no need to worry. It's just the local cows known to wander around the area with cowbells. This site is in Stanislaus National Forest. Free camping very close to the Big Oak Flat Entrance to Yosemite National Park!!

Photos: https://t2bk.com/ABK

136. SWEETWATER CAMPGROUND - $29/$14.50

- Stanislaus National Forest
- CA-120Groveland,
- GPS: 37.8239, -120.0051

Map: https://t2bk.com/ABL

Sweetwater Campground is located in a mixed conifer forest next to Highway 120 and is a stone's throw from Yosemite National Park. It's an ideal spot for exploring Yosemite, and additional day-use options are nearby. The campground offers basic dry campsites, most of which are open and sunny. Each site has a picnic table, a bear-proof storage box, and a fire pit with a grill. Accessible vault toilets and potable water are available from May to September in the summer.

This campground is quiet, and the sites are nicely spaced, offering some privacy. They're not all on level ground, but they're manageable. The bathrooms are kept clean. Not suitable for larger rigs.

Photos: https://t2bk.com/ABM

7
EASTERN CALIFORNIA

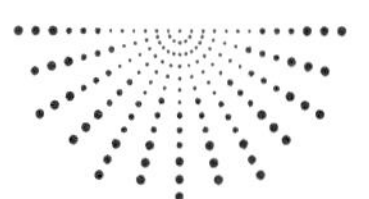

138. ALABAMA HILLS, MOVIE FLAT DESIGNATED DISPERSED CAMPING - FREE

- Alabama Hills Recreation Area
- BLM
- Lone Pine, CA
- GPS: 36.6054, -118.1189

Map: https://t2bk.com/ABN

Dispersed camping. This is not a campground. The Alabama Hills has spectacular views of Mt. Whitney and this unique desert area. Creeks and waterfalls are nearby. Hundreds of movies have been filmed in this area. Plan to stop at the film museum in Lone Pine.

Recent rule changes make this area more suitable for smaller rigs. Most of the areas that were suitable for bigger rigs are now designated as day use only. The following listing for Tuttle Creek is an excellent option for rigs of all sizes visiting this area. All sites are first-come, first-served. The cover photo for this book was taken here.

Photos; https://t2bk.com/ABO

139. TUTTLE CREEK CAMPGROUND - $10/$5

- BLM
- Horseshoe Meadow Rd.
- Lone Pine, CA
- GPS: 36.5723, -118.1095

Map: https://t2bk.com/ABQ

Tuttle Creek Campground is on the edge of the Alabama Hills and has incredible views of this unique desert area and Mt. Whitney. Tuttle Creek flows through the middle of the campground, and you can find many waterfalls nearby at Whitney Portal and on the way up the mountain. Hundreds of movies have been filmed in this area.

Tuttle Creek has 83 RV and tent sites, including ten pull-through spaces. It is suitable for RVs up to 30 feet in length. Each camping spot has a fire pit, picnic table, and lantern holder. No hook-ups are available. Potable water and clean vault toilets are available. There is good cell service. Plan to stop at the Western Film Museum in Lone Pine.

Photos: https://t2bk.com/ABR

140. GREEN CREEK ROAD DISPERSED CAMPING - FREE

- Toiyabe National Forest
- Green Creek Rd.
- Bridgeport, CA
- GPS: 38.1197, -119.2512

Map: https://t2bk.com/ABS

Green Creek Road dispersed camping is located in the Toiyabe National Forest near Austin, Nevada, offering seclusion within a high desert landscape carved by meadows and intermittent springs. The terrain features open sagebrush flats, scattered pinyon-juniper groves, and gently sloping hills. Spring-fed Green Creek runs nearby, attracting songbirds, deer, and the occasional antelope. While no marked trails begin at camp, forest roads and informal paths lead into adjacent hills and ridgelines, making it appealing for hiking, wildlife viewing, and nature photography.

Camping here is primitive with no designated campsites or amenities. The area accommodates tents and high-clearance trucks or RVs, accessible primarily via forest road. Camping is allowed year-round, with conditions changing by season.

Photos: https://t2bk.com/ABT

141. ASPEN CAMPGROUND - $14/$7

- Inyo National Forest
- Lee Vining, CA
- GPS: 37.939, -119.188

Map: https://t2bk.com/ABU

Aspen Campground is located along Lee Vining Creek in Inyo National Forest at about 7,500 feet elevation. The area is shaded by tall aspen, pine, and fir trees, with many sites close enough to hear the creek. The landscape is a mix of wooded slopes and grassy openings, offering partial views of the surrounding Sierra peaks. Wildlife such as mule deer, marmots, and mountain birds are commonly seen. Fishing for trout is popular along the creek, and several hiking trails in the area lead to alpine lakes and high-country scenery.

The campground has 45 drive-in sites, each with a picnic table, fire ring, and bear-proof food locker. Vault toilets are provided, but there is no potable water. All sites are first-come, first-served. The campground can become quite crowded during the summer, but it's a spectacular place to camp. The maximum length allowed for vehicles is 40 ft.

Photos: https://t2bk.com/ABV

142. GLASS CREEK CAMPGROUND - FREE

- Inyo National Forest
- Glass Creek Rd.
- June Lake, CA
- GPS: 37.7515, -118.9892

Map: https://t2bk.com/ABY

Glass Creek is a very nice free campground. It has a camp host, well-maintained vault toilets, and a good selection of roomy spots. The area has both shady and sunlit sites suitable for solar setups. A rest stop with flushable toilets and potable water is nearby.

The campground is accessible for RVs of all sizes and offers picnic tables, fire rings, and clean toilets. You'll find extensive trails beyond the campsite that are perfect for off-road enthusiasts. It's a 15-minute drive to either Mammoth or June Lake. There's no water or trash disposal at the campsite, but both are available at the nearby rest area.

Photos: https://t2bk.com/ABZ

143. LOWER LEE VINING CAMPGROUND - $14/$7

- Inyo National Forest
- Tioga Road
- Lee Vining, CA
- GPS: 37.9301, -119.1539

Map: https://t2bk.com/ACA

Near Yosemite! Lower Lee Vining Campground is open seasonally at an elevation of 7,300 feet. It offers 51 camping spots. There's no access to potable water in the campground, but about a mile west towards the park, you'll find a water filling station at a large pull-off area. Portable toilets are available. Each site includes a bear-proof locker for safe food storage for basic off-the-grid camping.

Bear Track Creek flows through this campground and is a popular fishing spot. The sites near the creek are notably large. The setting is breathtaking, and the restrooms are well-maintained. The Mobil station at Highways 395 and 120 offers a dump station and a good restaurant.

Photos: https://t2bk.com/ACB

144. OWENS RIVER RD DISPERSED CAMPING - FREE

- Inyo National Forest
- Owens River Rd.
- Mammoth Lakes, CA
- GPS: 37.737, -118.9677

Map: https://t2bk.com/ACE

This is not a campground. It is an outstanding spot for dispersed camping, and it can accommodate large rigs with various places to set up camp. There is excellent cell reception. You can park wherever you like in this dispersed camping area. Excellent sites are available on both sides of Owens River Road.

No facilities or amenities are available on-site, so being self-contained is essential. A rest stop just half a mile away has clean restrooms, trash dumpsters, and potable water. It's close to Mammoth Lakes and June Lake, and you can choose between shady areas or a sunny spot perfect for solar setups.

Photos: https://t2bk.com/ACF

145. CROWLEY LAKE CAMPGROUND - $10/$5

- BLM
- Crowley Lakes Drive
- Mammoth Lakes,
- GPS: 37.5717, -118.7666

Map: https://t2bk.com/ACG

Crowley Lake Campground has 47 sites suitable for RVs and tents. It's recommended that RVs not exceed 30 feet. Each site has a fire pit, picnic table, and a lantern holder, but there are no hook-ups. Visitors have access to potable water and well-maintained vault toilets. A dump station is available for a fee of $5.00. For additional amenities, the little town of Crowley is just 2 miles south, and Mammoth Lakes is about 10 miles north.

Thc campground has vicws of Crowley Lake and the Glass Mountains to the east, and the Sierra Nevada mountains and McGee Mountain and Canyon are the backdrop to the west. It's popular for fishing, boating, windsurfing, horseback riding, and hiking.

Photos: https://t2bk.com/ACH

146. MAMMOTH LAKES SCENIC LOOP – FREE

- Inyo National Forest
- Mammoth Scenic Loop Rd.
- Mammoth Lakes, CA
- GPS: 37.6839,-118.9946

Map: https://t2bk.com/ACI

Dispersed camping. This is not a campground. While not officially designated as a campground, many obvious camping spots are along both sides of the Scenic Loop. Mammoth Scenic Loop is popular for short-term and long-term stays. Some people stay out there for months while working seasonal jobs in town.

This is true dispersed camping in the national forest. There are no bathrooms, water, electricity, or fire rings. Remember that this area is an active bear area, and you won't find any bear box lockers. Have a method of locking up your food (like a bear-proof cooler) that isn't in your vehicle.

Photos: https://t2bk.com/ACJ

147. TABOOSE CREEK CAMPGROUND - $14

- County Park
- Tinemaha Rd. / Taboose Creek Rd.
- Independence, CA
- GPS: 36.9979, -118.2542

Map: https://t2bk.com/ACK

This is a lovely county park next to a creek. While it can get quite hot during the summer, plenty of smaller trees provide ample shade for setting up chairs or a tent. The park can accommodate any size rig and offers stunning views of the eastern Sierra.

Taboose Creek Campground is quiet and clean. It has vault toilets, picnic tables, grills, fire rings, stream fishing, 35 camp spaces, a water well, and can accommodate larger RVs. No shower facilities are available. Visitors can enjoy hiking on the excellent trails to stretch their legs or enjoy the views. Getting to the park is easy since it's only a mile from Hwy 395.

Photos: https://t2bk.com/ACL

148. SAGEHEN MEADOWS CAMPGROUND - FREE

- Inyo National Forest
- Forest Road 1N02A
- Mammoth Lakes, CA
- GPS: 37.8667, -118.8611

Map: https://t2bk.com/ACM

Dispersed camping. This is not a campground. Sagehen Meadows Campground in the Inyo National Forest is a hidden gem for boondockers. Waking up here means being greeted by the delightful scent of sage and the sweet butterscotch aroma of Jeffrey pines – it's truly an experience for the senses! Watch for the wild horses that sometimes roam around the area. The campground is easily accessible thanks to a usually well-maintained forest service road.

Autumn is beautiful, with the aspens painting the landscape in stunning fall colors. Facilities are minimal, with just a pit toilet available, but it's completely free and often peaceful due to its very low usage. This unspoiled camp area offers tranquility, majestic trees, a star-filled sky at night, local wildlife, and the refreshing mountain air. Plus, it's conveniently close to Mono Lake, Lee Vining, and Tioga Pass for those wanting to explore further.

Photos: https://t2bk.com/ACN

8
CENTRAL CALIFORNIA

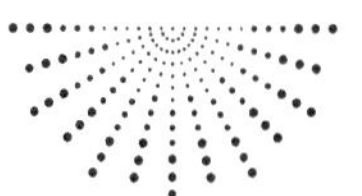

*** SEQUOIA & KINGS CANYON •••

150. PRINCESS CAMPGROUND - $34/$17

- Sequoia National Forest
- Highway 180
- Hume, CA
- GPS: 36.8027, -118.9412

Map: https://t2bk.com/ACY

This beautiful campground features three loops: Shining Cloud, Yellow Moon, and Morning Star. There's plenty of shade throughout the site, and privacy varies from fair to good between campsites. Princess Campground is in the heart of Indian Basin Grove, adjacent to Indian Basin Meadow and Creek. It is situated in the Sequoia National Forest and enjoys a cooler climate, even during the warm summer months.

The campground is enveloped by tall trees, with certain areas opening to a vast meadow. At night, the gaps in the treetops create a natural window to the sky above. The forest provides a perfect balance of shade and space so that you can see the starry night sky. Open year-round. First-come, first-served.

Photos: https://t2bk.com/ACZ

151. WESTERN BIG MEADOW ROAD CAMPING AREA - FREE

- Sequoia National Forest
- FR-14S11
- Hume, CA
- GPS: 36.7116, -118.8569

Map: https://t2bk.com/ADA

Dispersed camping. This is not a campground. This excellent free camping area provides easy access to Sequoia and Kings Canyon National Parks. You'll find many camping spots along the road, offering a peaceful and picturesque setting in the woods. This is terrific dispersed camping, with plenty of room to accommodate all sizes of rigs.

Photos: https://t2bk.com/ADB

The road to the area is paved, ensuring easy access to the national parks. Surrounded by forests, there are numerous roads to explore for those seeking adventure. There are pit toilets near the picnic area at the road's entrance. The area has many large, level sites perfect for dispersed camping, including several spots with stunning granite slabs for basking in the sunshine. Note that more free and paid camping areas are to the east on Big Meadow Road.

152. REDWOOD MEADOW CAMPGROUND - $34/$17

- Sequoia National Forest
- Great Western Divide Highway
- Porterville, CA 93257
- GPS: 35.977, -118.592

Map: https://t2bk.com/ADC

This beautiful campground, about 50 miles east of Springville, CA, offers a serene experience. There are vault toilets, but no water, so bring what you'll need. A highlight is the 100 Giants Trail across the road, which features excellent walking trails. For a unique stay, yurts are available for rent at $100 a night.

The campground is known for its quiet and idyllic setting, complete with friendly little critters around. It has excellent views, and campsites have fire pits with grills. Nearby, you'll find great hiking. Most campsites are small, so it's more suitable for small RVs and tent campers. Popular campground.

Photos: https://t2bk.com/ADD

153. UPPER STONY CREEK CAMPGROUND - $34/$17

- Sequoia National Forest
- FR-14S21
- Sequoia National Park, CA
- GPS: 36.668, -118.829

Map: https://t2bk.com/ADE

Upper Stony Creek campground, located 14 miles southeast of Grant Grove on Generals Highway, has sites for RVs and tents. It also has vault toilets, a picnic area, and drinking water. The campground is a good base for hiking into the Jennie Lakes Wilderness or mountain biking in the surrounding areas.

Photos: https://t2bk.com/ADF

Just half a mile away, Stony Creek Resort offers a range of amenities, including a public phone, showers, groceries, Wi-Fi, a restaurant, and gasoline. The drive to the campground can be a bit bumpy. With only 11 sites, the campground feels spacious and quiet. A small river runs near the site, and you can hear the sound of the water at night. It's just 20 minutes from Sequoia National Park.

9
SOUTHERN CALIFORNIA

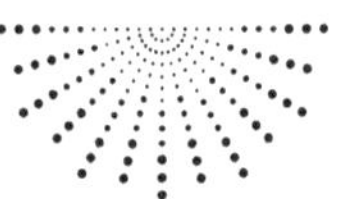

••• MOJAVE DESERT •••

155. SILURIAN DRY LAKE BED - FREE

- BLM
- Death Valley Rd,
- Baker, CA
- GPS: 35.5266, -116.1785

Map: https://t2bk.com/AEX

Dispersed camping. This is not a campground. Camping at Silurian Dry Lake Bed is like stepping into a world of stunning desolation. It's the perfect spot for boondocking, offering a peaceful retreat in the desert. You're surrounded by breathtaking views that make this a unique experience. Be aware, though, that the desert wind can sometimes be a challenge.

Every sunrise and sunset here can be a spectacular show, and the sky is a blanket of stars at night. The silence is profound. If you're lucky, you might see some wild burros. This place is a dream for those who cherish solitude and want to escape it all. There's also plenty to explore nearby, including old turquoise mines, if you do some research to see where they are.

Photos: https://t2bk.com/AEY

156. TRONA PINNACLES - FREE

- BLM
- Trona, CA
- GPS: 35.619, -117.37

Map: https://t2bk.com/AEZ

Dispersed camping. This is not a campground. The Trona Pinnacles are a marvel of surreal natural beauty in an almost alien landscape. This extraordinary area features over 500 tufa spires, some towering as high as 140 feet, emerging from the Searles Dry Lake floor. Recognizing its unique geological value, the Trona Pinnacles were designated a National Natural Landmark in 1968 by the U.S. Department of the Interior, celebrated as one of North America's most remarkable examples of tufa tower formations.

This unearthly landscape offers an incredible camping, hiking, or off-roading setting. The area is laced with hiking and off-roading trails, which are great for exploration. The Pinnacles can get quite busy on weekends. As of this writing, the smoother access road is from the north via Highway 178 from Searles Valley.

Photos: https://t2bk.com/AFA

157. OWL CANYON CAMPGROUND - $6/$3

- BLM Rainbow Basin Natural Area
- Rainbow-Basin
- Barstow, CA
- GPS: 35.0213, -117.0217

Map: https://t2bk.com/AFB

Own Canyon Campground in Rainbow Basin has a mix of hills, canyons, and washes, making it a hub for various activities like hiking, camping, photography, sightseeing, and horseback riding. The area is known for its multi-colored rock walls and mesas, providing plenty of opportunities for photographers. The washes serve as excellent hiking trails. This prime spot for desert boondocking offers large sites and is conveniently located near pit toilets, making it an ideal destination for an overnight stay.

While the 5-mile journey on a washboard dirt road might be challenging, the beautiful desert landscapes waiting at the end make it worthwhile. Each campsite has a fire pit, grill, and covered picnic table. The vault toilets are kept clean, and the sites are generously sized, accommodating everything from tents to larger rigs.

Photos: https://t2bk.com/AFC

158. KELSO DUNES MINE - FREE

- Mojave National Preserve
- Kelso-Dunes Road
- Amboy, CA
- GPS: 34.8881, -115.7166

Map: https://t2bk.com/AFD

Dispersed camping. This is not a campground. This location near the Kelso Dunes is a fantastic boondocking find. It's the perfect place to see the sunrise and sunset over the dunes. While there's no shade, the area's beauty is magical. The ample space has enough room to accommodate multiple vehicles and offers incredible views of the dunes. Pit toilets are available.

The dunes themselves, along with the views and night sky, are breathtaking. Getting there might test your patience due to the road conditions, but the destination is worth the effort. You'll love this spot if you enjoy wide-open spaces and stunning sunrises. It's suitable for rigs of all sizes.

Photos: https://t2bk.com/AFE

159. MID HILLS CAMPGROUND - $20/$10

- Mojave National Preserve
- Wild Horse Canyon Rd.
- Cima, CA
- GPS: 35.1299, -115.4354

Map: https://t2bk.com/AFF

Mid Hills Campground, located at 5,600 feet among pinyon pines and juniper trees, offers an escape from the desert heat below. The unpaved access road is rough, making it unsuitable for larger motorhomes or trailers. It is best for higher-clearance vehicles. The campground has pit toilets, trash receptacles, fire rings, and picnic tables.

It is very secluded and has fantastic views. It has a quiet and peaceful atmosphere. Beautiful sunrises and sunsets, as well as the moon and starry night sky, are breathtaking. The restrooms are well-maintained, and the juniper trees and desert flora provide privacy between the large sites. Cima Dome and the Kelso Dunes recreation areas are nearby.

Photos: https://t2bk.com/AFG

160. FOSSIL FALLS DRY LAKE BED - FREE

- BLM
- Cinder Road
- Little Lake, CA
- GPS: 35.9828, -117.9004

Map: https://t2bk.com/AFH

Dispersed camping. This is not a campground. Fossil Falls Dry Lake Bed is next to the BLM Fossil Falls Recreation Area, which offers stunning scenic views. After exiting the paved road, you will travel a few hundred yards on a bumpy but hard-packed road. You can choose where to set up camp when you reach the lake bed. Very few people use this area.

Although summer can be hot, the rest of the year has pleasant weather. You can also take a leisurely walk to see the Fossil Falls. The cell service at this location is excellent.

Photos: https://t2bk.com/AFI

161. AMBOY CRATER - FREE

- BLM Mojave Trails National Monument
- Crater Road
- Amboy, CA
- GPS: 34.5577, -115.7769

Map: https://t2bk.com/AFJ

Amboy Crater, an iconic landscape of ash and cinders, is one of the United States' youngest volcanic fields. It stands 250 feet tall and has a diameter of 1,500 feet. Just off Old Route 66, this site has picnic tables, restroom facilities, and an ADA-compliant ramada overlook for scenic viewing. There's a hiking trail to the rim, complete with rest stations along the way. The area is very quiet except for the occasional passing train in the distance.

The road is easy to navigate in vehicles of any size. Waking up to the lunar-like landscape is a unique experience. The location is exceptionally dark and fantastic for quiet stargazing. The large and level parking lot is perfect for a night under the stars. There are covered picnic tables and two bathrooms with pit toilets on-site. It can get quite hot in the summer but is pleasant the rest of the year.

Photos: https://t2bk.com/AFK

••• DEATH VALLEY AREA •••

162. WILDROSE CAMPGROUND - FREE

- Death Valley National Park
- 24 Wildrose Canyon Rd.
- Death Valley, CA
- GPS: 36.2657, -117.1905

Map: https://t2bk.com/AFN

Wildrose Campground is a beautiful spot to camp in Death Valley. The campsites are small and high enough in elevation not to be too warm, but no shade is available. Two roads lead up to the campsite. Emigrant Road has a 25-foot maximum tow restriction. The road is easy until right before the campground when it gets twisty and tight. Wildrose Road is shorter but only partially paved.

The road is rugged and not suited to bigger rigs. However, you'll enjoy the gorgeous night sky and vast open space. There are clean bathrooms, water, and trash cans, and each site has a picnic table and spectacular views. There are 23 campsites, and they are available on a first-come, first-served basis.

Photos: https://t2bk.com/AFO

163. STOVEPIPE WELLS CAMPGROUND - $14/$7

- Death Valley National Park
- Cottonwood Canyon Rd.
- Stovepipe Wells, CA
- GPS: 36.6068, -117.1478

Map: https://t2bk.com/AFP

Enjoy basic camping in the heart of a magnificent National Park, available seasonally from October 15th. Stovepipe Wells campground is at sea level and operates on a first-come, first-served basis. It offers scenic views of Death Valley and the Mesquite Flat Sand Dunes. The campground is next to the Stovepipe Wells general store, a ranger station, and a privately run RV park.

Stovepipe Wells Campground offers dry camping in a large parking area and has flush toilets, trash and recycling bins, dump station access, and potable water refilling. For those interested in hiking, the nearby dunes are a fantastic spot for a morning or evening adventure.

Photos: https://t2bk.com/AFQ

164. FURNACE CREEK ROAD DISPERSED CAMPING - FREE

- BLM
- Furnace Creek Washington Rd.
- Shoshone, CA
- GPS: 35.9061, -116.2968

Map: https://t2bk.com/AFR

Dispersed camping. This is not a campground. South of Death Valley, off of Hwy 127, is an excellent area for stargazing and boondocking. It offers privacy and spaciousness, with room between campsites. The landscapes and views here are breathtaking, with beautiful sunrises and sunsets. There's ample parking available on solid, rocky ground in a beautiful, open area. The terrain is pretty level and clean, but there's no shade.

The nights are quiet, perfect for enjoying the expansive sky views. There are no amenities. The dirt road leading to the camp area is well-maintained. The area's landscape and geology offer endless hiking opportunities and rockhounding. The Tecopa hot springs are nearby, as is the China Date Ranch and their delicious date smoothies and shakes.

Photos: https://t2bk.com/AFS

••• JOSHUA TREE AREA •••

165. JOSHUA TREE SOUTH DISPERSED CAMPING - FREE

- BLM
- Cottonwood Spring Rd.
- Chiriaco Summit, CA
- GPS: 33.6745, -115.8019

Map: https://t2bk.com/AFT

Dispersed camping. This is not a campground. Joshua Tree South is located a mile from the Cottonwood Springs Rd. exit off I-10, and the lack of road noise makes for a quiet stay. It's only a few miles to Joshua Tree National Park's southern entrance, and there's excellent cell service. The area is gorgeous in the spring when wildflowers bloom. The transformation of the desert during that time of year is breathtaking.

The area can accommodate rigs of all sizes. Despite the bumpy dirt road, it's easy to navigate to this location with a regular car. There are no facilities here, but there is a dump station at Joshua Tree NP's Cottonwood campground. Great for star gazing.

Photos: https://t2bk.com/AFU

166. BELLE CAMPGROUND - $25/$12.50

- Joshua Tree National Park
- Belle Campground Rd.
- Twentynine Palms, CA
- GPS: 34.0021, -116.021

Map: https://t2bk.com/AFV

Belle Campground is small, with 18 sites and first-come, first-served. Be sure to bring plenty of your own water, as none is available on-site, though pit toilets are provided. This campground is great for stargazing, thanks to the dark night skies it offers. The campsites are cleverly situated among the rocks, creating a picturesque Joshua Tree setting with large granite boulders and the iconic Joshua trees dotting the landscape.

It's smaller, more secluded, and quieter than other Joshua Tree campgrounds. Its central location offers easy access to many of the park's main attractions. The area is known for its incredible sunsets and sunrises, breathtaking starry skies, beautiful rock formations, and the call of coyotes at night.

Photos: https://t2bk.com/AFW

10
NEVADA

168. THOMAS CANYON CAMPGROUND - $19/$9.50

- Humboldt-Toiyabe National Forest
- NF-660
- Spring Creek, NV
- GPS: 40.6509, -115.4071

Map: https://t2bk.com/AOE

Thomas Canyon Campground sits in the upper reaches of Lamoille Canyon, surrounded by the dramatic peaks of the Ruby Mountains. The steep canyon walls are dotted with aspens, pines, and seasonal wildflowers, especially vibrant in early summer. Lamoille Creek runs through the area, providing a natural soundtrack and occasional wildlife sightings—deer and marmots are common, and birdlife is active throughout the warmer months. The nearby trailhead connects directly to popular hikes like the Thomas Canyon Trail and access into the Ruby Crest Trail network, known for alpine lakes, granite ridges, and panoramic views.

The campground has 16 sites, each outfitted with a picnic table and fire ring, and is suitable for both tents and small to mid-sized RVs. There are vault toilets and garbage service, but no hookups. Sites are first-come, first-served, and the campground is typically open from late spring through early fall.

Photos: https://t2bk.com/AOG

169. VALLEY OF FIRE WEST DISPERSED CAMPING - FREE

- BLM
- Valley of Fire Highway
- Overton, NV
- GPS: 36.4445, -114.6756

Map: https://t2bk.com/AOF

The closest boondocking to Las Vegas and very close to the entrance to Valley of Fire State Park. This area offers stunning and expansive views, with the distant Mt. Charleston visible on the horizon and beautiful sunsets to enjoy. The gravel roads make for easy navigation, and it's a great spot to spend a few nights while exploring the Valley of Fire.

Photos: https://t2bk.com/AOH

This is dispersed camping with no developed sites, so you'll be parking on hardened surfaces or pulling into cleared patches. There are no restrooms, water, or trash service, so you'll need to be fully self-contained. It is open year-round, with no reservations required. If you need supplies, the Moapa Travel Center is just 6 miles away and offers a variety of amenities, including a store, casino, fireworks, restaurant, gas, diesel, restrooms, water, and dumpsters.

170. WILSON CANYON - FREE

- BLM
- Highway 208
- Yerington, NV
- GPS: 38.8076, -119.2231

Map: https://t2bk.com/AOI

Wilson Canyon is a narrow gorge carved by the Walker River as it cuts through volcanic rock formations between Smith Valley and Yerington, Nevada. The area is dry and rocky, surrounded by rugged hills dotted with desert shrubs like sagebrush and rabbitbrush. The river runs seasonally, attracting birds and the occasional mule deer. The landscape includes steep cliffs and boulder-strewn slopes, with a few informal footpaths and ATV tracks along the canyon floor. The region is popular with hikers, photographers, and off-road enthusiasts looking for solitude and stark beauty.

There are no developed campgrounds in the canyon itself, but dispersed camping is available in flat pullouts along the dirt access road. There are no facilities, so you must be fully self-sufficient. The area is accessible most of the year, but can be muddy after storms or snowmelt.

Photos: https://t2bk.com/AOJ

171. WATER CANYON RECREATION AREA - FREE

- BLM
- Water Canyon Rd.
- Winnemucca, NV
- GPS: 40.9295, -117.6736

Map: https://t2bk.com/AOK

Water Canyon Recreation Area is just east of Winnemucca, Nevada, where desert meets mountains in a scenic high-desert setting. Rocky hillsides, sparse juniper trees, and views of the Santa Rosa Range to the north define the area. Water Canyon Creek flows seasonally through the canyon, and cottonwoods grow along its banks. This is a popular spot for hiking, mountain biking, and wildlife viewing—especially mule deer and various birds. A few rough trails climb into the hills, providing expansive views of the valley below.

The area offers a mix of developed and dispersed camping options. Several gravel pull-through sites are available, with picnic tables and fire rings. Vault toilets are on site, but there is no potable water or trash service. First-come, first-served, and the area is generally accessible most of the year. Camping is limited to a maximum of 3 days per month.

Photos: https://t2bk.com/AOL

172. BOB SCOTT CAMPGROUND - $10/$5

- Toiyabe National Forest
- Lincoln Highway
- Austin, NV
- GPS: 39.4565, -116.9944

Map: https://t2bk.com/AOM

This clean high desert campground is a beautiful destination for camping enthusiasts. With facilities such as picnic tables, toilets, and drinking water, visitors can expect a comfortable stay, whether they are in tents or camping trailers. The campground is generally open from May to October, depending on weather conditions. Bob Scott Summit, surrounded by a pinyon-juniper forest, is easily accessible from U.S. Route 50.

Hunting for deer and elk is a popular activity during the appropriate seasons. Another option is fishing at Birch Creek, only 8 miles from the campground. Restrooms and water are available, but trash cans are not provided, so campers should pack out their garbage.

Photos: https://t2bk.com/AON

173. GREAT BASIN WILDLIFE CROSSING - FREE

- BLM
- Great Basin Highway 93
- Wells, NV 89835
- GPS: 41.2061, -114.8535

Maps: https://t2bk.com/AOU

Great Basin Wildlife Crossing near Wells, Nevada, is a dispersed camping spot just off Highway 93. It's a gravel pull-off and also has backroad access into juniper-dotted terrain. The land is open and gently sloping, with scattered trees and views of nearby ranges. Wildlife sightings include mule deer crossing the area at dusk, and birdlife is frequent around the edges of the flat sites. Since the site lies along a highway corridor, occasional vehicle noise is expected, but you can probably find quieter spots further from the road. This is a convenient spot if you need to take a break or get some sleep overnight.

Camping here is undeveloped. There are no marked sites, no toilets, no potable water, and no garbage service. You'll find room for tents, vans, and trailers in the open gravel areas and cleared patches. All camping is first-come, first-served year-round. Some users note a gate that may be closed—check locally.

Photos: https://t2bk.com/AOV

174. ANGEL CREEK CAMPGROUND - $17/$8.50

Humboldt-Toiyabe National Forest

- NF-098
- Wells, NV
- GPS: 41.0287, -115.0509

Map: https://t2bk.com/AOO

Angel Creek Campground sits in a scenic pine-forested valley within the East Humboldt Range of northeastern Nevada. The area is surrounded by high alpine peaks, with aspen, spruce, and fir trees providing shade and cool air in summer. Angel Lake lies just up the road, offering fishing and paddling, and several hiking trails branch out toward the rugged mountain ridges and alpine lakes above. Wildlife such as deer, marmots, and various birds are commonly spotted.

The campground has 19 sites spaced among trees, with gravel pads, picnic tables, and fire rings. Vault toilets and trash bins are available, but there is no potable water. Sites are first-come, first-served, and are generally open from late spring through early fall, depending on weather and snowmelt. It's located just below Angel Lake and Angel Lake Campground, making it an excellent base camp for fishing and hiking.

Photos: https://t2bk.com/AOP

175. HICKISON PETROGLYPH RECREATION AREA - FREE

- BLM
- Lincoln Highway
- Austin, NV 89310
- GPS: 39.4493, -116.7514

Maps: https://t2bk.com/APA

Hickison Petroglyph Recreation Area is on U.S. Highway 50 in central Nevada, in the high desert at about 6,500 feet elevation. The site is surrounded by piñon-juniper and sagebrush habitat, with expansive views across the Big Smoky Valley and nearby mountain ranges. A short interpretive loop trail leads to multiple rock walls bearing prehistoric petroglyphs. Birds of prey, small mammals, and desert flora are typical in the area.

The campground includes 16 designated sites along a dirt loop, each with a picnic table, fire ring, grill, and parking spur. Vault toilets and trash receptacles are available, but there is no potable water or hookups. All sites are first-come, first-served; reservations are not accepted. Open year-round, though access may vary seasonally. The layout accommodates tents, trucks, vans, and smaller RVs, and large rigs may find some turns tight.

Photos: https://t2bk.com/APB

176. GEMFIELD ROAD DISPERSED CAMPING - FREE

- BLM
- Gemfield Rd.
- Goldfield, NV 89013
- GPS: 37.74, -117.2611

Maps: https://t2bk.com/APC

Gemfield Road Dispersed Camping lies just east of Goldfield, Nevada, in a high desert valley framed by rugged hills and distant mountain ranges. The terrain is mostly flat and open, with patches of sagebrush, rabbitbrush, and scattered juniper. Though there are no formal trails that begin at camp, nearby dirt roads and old mining tracks offer routes to explore ridgelines, washes, and historic sites. Wildlife such as pronghorn, jackrabbits, and raptors are often seen, especially in the morning and evening.

This is truly primitive camping—there are no designated sites, vault toilets, water, or trash services. You'll find cleared pull-outs and patches of level ground that are suitable for tents, campers, vans, and smaller RVs. Camping is first-come, first-served. The area remains accessible most of the year and is popular with those seeking solitude near Goldfield's mining relics and wide open skies.

Photos: https://t2bk.com/APD

177. BONNIE CLAIRE LAKEBED - FREE

- BLM
- Scotty's Castle Rd. (NV-267)
- Beatty, NV 89003
- GPS: 37.1709, -117.1519

Maps:
https://t2bk.com/APE

Bonnie Claire Lakebed sits in a stark, open desert basin shaped by a dry lakebed surface. It's secluded and very quiet. You'll see flat expanses bordered by low hills and distant mountain ridgelines. Vegetation is sparse—mainly creosote, sagebrush, and occasional scrub—so the terrain feels broad and exposed. While there are no formal trails from camp, old mining roads, washes, and open terrain invite exploration. Wildlife such as jackrabbits, sidewinders, and raptors may pass through during early or late hours.

Camping here is fully dispersed—with no marked sites, restrooms, water, or trash facilities. You'll find wide room to park a tent, van, or RV on the hardened clay or gravel surface. All use is first-come, first-served, and no reservations are accepted. The lakebed is open year-round. ***Be aware that after rain, the clay surface can become soft or muddy.***

Photos:
https://t2bk.com/APF

178. INDIAN SPRINGS VALLEY DISPERSED CAMPING - FREE

- BLM
- FR-553
- Mercury, NV 89023
- GPS: 36.574, -115.8789

Maps: https://t2bk.com/APG

Indian Springs Valley Dispersed Camping is near Mercury, Nevada, just off Forest Road 553. This is open desert with gravel washes, low shrubs, and scattered creosote and sagebrush. Nearby ridges and distant peaks frame the landscape, giving a broad view of the surrounding basin. Wildlife here is sparse, but you might see jackrabbits, coyotes, or desert birds. There are no formal hiking trails here, though adjacent BLM roads and washes invite exploration on foot or by vehicle.

This is a primitive, dispersed camping area with no designated sites or facilities. There are cleared pull-outs with gravel surfaces that can accommodate tents, vans, or equipped RVs. There are no toilets, water sources, or trash service. Camping is first-come, first-served, with no reservations accepted, and the area is generally accessible year-round.

Photos: https://t2bk.com/APH

179. FISH LAKE VALLEY HOT WELL - FREE

- County Park
- Dyer, NV 89010
- GPS: 37.8602, -117.9839

Maps: https://t2bk.com/API

Fish Lake Valley Hot Well (also called Fish Lake Hot Springs) is near Dyer, Nevada, tucked into the wide high-desert basin. The setting is open and expansive, with distant White Mountains framing the view. A concrete soaking tub flows from a hot geothermal source, and overflow trickles into a series of natural ponds. Marshy edges around the ponds draw birds and wetland vegetation. Wildlife in the area includes ducks, coots, and small fish (notably goldfish) in the ponds, while desert species roam in the surrounding sagebrush flats.

Dispersed camping is allowed in the large parking area and surrounding clearings, offering room for tents, vans, and RVs. There is a vault toilet nearby, but no potable water or hookups. Camping is first-come, first-served. The hot spring is accessible year-round, and most campers spread out from the tub to preserve space and privacy.

Photos: https://t2bk.com/APJ

180. ANGEL LAKE CAMPGROUND - $18/$9

- Humboldt-Toiyabe National Forest
- NF-098 / Angel Lake Rd.
- Wells, NV
- GPS: 41.027, -115.0835

***CAUTION - VERY STEEP WINDING ROAD** up to the lake and campground.*

Map: https://t2bk.com/AOQ

Angel Lake Campground sits high in the East Humboldt Mountains of northeastern Nevada, just below Angel Lake at around 8,400 feet. The alpine setting is rich with spruce, aspen, and fir, offering dense shade and a cooler escape in summer. The steep peaks surrounding the lake are striking, and trails nearby include the Winchell Lake Trail and Smith Lake Trail. The lake is small but quite scenic, with trout fishing and calm water for paddling. Deer and marmots are frequently seen, and the area draws both campers and day visitors.

The campground has 26 sites arranged along a loop, with tables, fire rings, and tent or small trailer pads. Vault toilets are provided, but there is no potable water. First-come, first-served. Open seasonally, typically late spring to early fall, depending on snowpack.

Photos: https://t2bk.com/AOR

181. TWENTY MILE BEACH - FREE

- Walker Lake Recreation Area
- Veterans Memorial Hwy. Hwy 95
- Hawthorne, NV 89415
- GPS: 38.752, -118.7655

Maps: https://t2bk.com/APK

Twenty Mile Beach lies along the western shore of Walker Lake, offering a wide lakeside setting framed by desert hills and distant peaks. The shoreline is primarily sandy and gravelly, with scattered shrubs and minimal tree cover. While there are no formal trails from the camping edge, you can walk along the lake's edge or explore the surrounding terrain using unpaved roads. Birdlife is present, and raptors and waterfowl may be visible near the water.

Camping at Twenty Mile Beach is primitive and relatively undeveloped. There are no designated campsites, but a gravel network of pull-offs and loops provides space for tents and RVs. A single vault toilet is available, but there is no potable water, no hookups, and no trash service. Access is first-come, first-served, and the area is generally open year-round. Do not camp in the day use area.

Photos: https://t2bk.com/APL

182. CLEVE CREEK CAMPGROUND - FREE

- Humboldt-Toiyabe National Forest
- National Forest Development Road 435
- Ely, NV 89301
- GPS: 39.2192, -114.5584

Maps: https://t2bk.com/AOW

Cleve Creek Campground lies along a year-round stream shaded by mature cottonwood and poplar trees, tucked into a scenic canyon off State Route 893 near Ely, Nevada. The camp is framed by the foothills of the Schell Creek Range, offering pleasant walk-in access to creekside views and forested slopes. Wildlife such as mule deer and songbirds frequent the riparian zone, and the sound of flowing water is a constant backdrop. The terrain is generally level, though scattered rocks and roots require attention when choosing a pad.

The campground includes 12 individual sites and one group site, all equipped with picnic tables, fire rings, and grills. Vault toilets are present, but there is no potable water. Some sites feature pull-through access, but large trailers may find maneuvering tight. All sites are first-come, first-served, and the campground is typically open in the warmer months.

Photos: https://t2bk.com/AOX

183. PATTERSON PASS CAMPGROUND - FREE

- BLM
- Patterson Pass Road
- Pioche, NV 89043
- GPS: 38.5921, -114.6671

Maps: https://t2bk.com/AOY

Patterson Pass Campground is just off Patterson Pass Road west of Pioche, Nevada, at an elevation of about 6,165 feet. The terrain is semi-arid and mostly open, with scattered juniper and sagebrush offering patchy shade. You'll find rugged hills surrounding the site, and the campground serves as a trailhead for the Silver State OHV Trail System, giving good access for off-highway exploration. Birds, small mammals, and desert flora are common sightings, especially near dawn and dusk.

The campground has 12 gravel sites, ranging from tent-sized to ones that can handle larger rigs, with some pull-throughs. Each site has a picnic table, fire ring, barbecue grill, and several shade structures. Vault toilets and trash disposal are available, but there is no potable water. All sites are first-come, first-served. The campground is open year-round and used by campers and OHV riders alike.

Photos: https://t2bk.com/AOZ

184. WHEELER PEAK CAMPGROUND - $20/$10

- Great Basin National Park
- Wheeler Peak Scenic Dr.
- Baker, NV
- GPS: 39.0107, -114.3044

Map: https://t2bk.com/AOS

Wheeler Peak Campground is below Wheeler Peak at around 9,800 feet. Surrounded by subalpine forest with stands of Engelmann spruce and bristlecone pine, the area offers sweeping views of Nevada's rugged Snake Range. Popular nearby trails include the Alpine Lakes Loop, Bristlecone Trail, and the longer Wheeler Peak Summit Trail. Wildlife sightings may include mule deer, marmots, and pikas, especially early mornings.

Photos: https://t2bk.com/AOT

The campground has 37 sites arranged in multiple loops, suitable for tents or smaller RVs. Facilities include picnic tables, fire rings, and vault toilets. There is no dump station, and potable water is typically available only in the summer months. The campground operates seasonally, usually from June to late September, depending on snow levels. All sites are first-come, first-served. The access road is steep and not recommended for vehicles over 24 feet.

185. VIRGIN VALLEY CAMPGROUND - FREE

- Sheldon National Wildlife Refuge
- Sage Brush Rd.
- Denio, NV 89404
- GPS: 41.8534, -119.0021

Maps: https://t2bk.com/APM

Virgin Valley Campground at Sheldon National Wildlife Refuge is set in high desert sagebrush terrain, with views of rugged hills and distant mountain ridgelines. Spring-fed ponds and warm springs are located nearby, offering natural soaking opportunities. Wildlife like pronghorn antelope, mule deer, and various bird species are common, especially near the water sources and open flats. Scattered juniper, sagebrush, and low shrubs dot the campground and surrounding area.

The campground has 15 sites, each with a picnic table and fire ring. Vault toilets and a rustic shower house fed from the warm springs are available, and potable water is provided seasonally. Camping is first-come, first-served—reservations are not accepted. The sites accommodate tents, vans, and modest RVs. The campground is open year-round, with seasonal closures and service variations in the colder months.

Photos: https://t2bk.com/APN

186. BIG DUNE DISPERSED CAMPING - FREE

- BLM
- Big Dunes Rd.
- Amargosa Valley, NV 89020
- GPS: 36.6447, -116.6092

Maps: https://t2bk.com/APO

Big Dune sits in a wide desert basin dotted with rolling sand hills rising up to five square miles of dunes. The terrain is a mix of hard-packed flats, soft sands, and scattered creosote and sagebrush. While there aren't formal trails from camp, the area is criss-crossed by OHV tracks for dune riding and exploration. Wildlife sightings may include lizards, jackrabbits, and raptors riding thermals overhead.

Photos: https://t2bk.com/APP

You can set up camp across the area's open spaces—there are no marked pads, restrooms, or water sources. Pull-outs and cleared spots along the dunes offer room for tents, vans, and smaller RVs. Camping is allowed year-round, on a first-come, first-served basis. The surrounding dune field sees frequent off-road activity, so consider placing your camp slightly back from the busiest tracks.

187. SOUTH RUBY CAMPGROUND - $17/$8.50

- Humboldt-Toiyabe National Forest
- Ruby Valley Road
- Elko, NV
- GPS: 40.176, -115.496

Maps: https://t2bk.com/ATE

South Ruby Campground is just above the edge of Ruby Lake in Nevada, framed by the forested slopes of the Ruby Mountains. The terrain transitions from sagebrush flats into groves of pinyon pine and juniper, and the nearby marshes make this area a notable spot for birds—canvasbacks, trumpeter swans, and sandhill cranes frequent the lake and its wetland fringes. You'll also see mule deer, pronghorn antelope, and other high-desert wildlife in the meadows and uplands.

The campground offers thirty-five sites, one double unit, and an accessible site—all with picnic tables, fire rings, and parking spurs. Vault toilets and drinking water are provided during the main summer season. Sites are available by reservation during peak months and revert to first-come availability in the off-season. A lower loop often remains open year-round even when the upper loop is closed.

Photos: https://t2bk.com/ATF

188. WARD MOUNTAIN CAMPGROUND - $12/$6

- Humboldt-Toiyabe National Forest
- Ward Mountain Rd.
- Ruth, NV 89319
- GPS: 39.2135, -114.969

Photos: https://t2bk.com/ATG

Ward Mountain Campground sits in a mixed pinyon and juniper forest near Ely, Nevada, offering a scenic base beneath the slopes of Ward Mountain. You'll find short hiking and biking trails leaving from or near the campground, with views of rolling hills, forested ridges, and high-desert valleys. Wildlife such as mule deer and various birds use the forest edge and open meadows.

The campground includes 33 individual and several group sites, all with picnic tables, fire rings, and grills. Vault toilets and potable water are provided, though no electric hookups are available. Sites can accommodate tents, trailers, and RVs up to roughly 40 feet in length. Many sites can be reserved, while some are first-come, first-served. The campground is typically open from late spring through early fall.

Photos: https://t2bk.com/ATH

11
ARIZONA

190. GARLAND PRAIRIE ROAD DISPERSED CAMPING - FREE

- Kaibab National Forest
- Garland Prairie Rd.
- Williams, AZ
- GPS: 35.2878, -112.1334

Map: https://t2bk.com/APQ

Near the Grand Canyon. Garland Prairie Road Dispersed Camping is set within a patchwork of meadows and ponderosa pine forest south of Williams, Arizona. It's a peaceful, open setting often visited by elk, deer, and various birds. Access to the Sycamore Rim Trail and other Kaibab National Forest routes is nearby, offering hiking and nature-viewing opportunities. Sunsets can be dramatic over the open prairie and distant hills.

The campsite is accessible via a dirt road, but it could get muddy during the rainy season. Campers can set up in a wooded area or an open field. There are no facilities—no toilets, water, or trash service—so you must be fully self-contained. Sites vary in size and privacy, with some accommodating larger rigs. The area is accessible from spring through fall, depending on snowmelt.

Photos: https://t2bk.com/APR

191. SCHOOLHOUSE CAMPGROUND - $20/$10

- Tonto National Forest
- Point Rd.
- Roosevelt, AZ 85545
- GPS: 33.6416, -111.0078

Maps:
https://t2bk.com/ARS

Schoolhouse Campground is just above the eastern shore of Roosevelt Lake at about 2,100 feet elevation, surrounded by Sonoran Desert terrain with mesquite trees and distant mountains. A short lakeside trail provides gentle walking through the native vegetation to viewpoints of the water, and anglers often frequent the shore for bass and catfish. Wildlife like quail, rabbits, and various desert birds are common, especially near the vegetation edge.

Photos:
https://t2bk.com/ART

The campground has 40 paved sites arranged in the Mesquite Loop, each with a picnic table, fire ring with grill, and pull-through pad suited for RVs up to around 32 feet. Vault toilets are available, but there is no potable water on site. Odd-numbered sites may be reserved between November 1 and April 30; even-numbered sites are first-come, first-served year-round. Seasonal access is generally maintained throughout the year. Note: The campground may close at very low lake levels.

192. CHRISTOPHER CREEK CAMPGROUND - $24/$12

- Tonto National Forest
- Hwy 260
- Payson, AZ 85541
- GPS: 34.3128, -111.0389

Maps: https://t2bk.com/ARU

Christopher Creek Campground sits along spring-fed Christopher Creek just beneath the rim country near Payson, Arizona. The setting is shaded by ponderosa pines, junipers, and oaks, with forested slopes rising toward the Mogollon Rim. Hikers can follow nearby paths into side canyons or explore the rim trails above. Wildlife includes mule deer, songbirds, and occasionally brook or brown trout in the creek.

The campground has 43 individual campsites plus a group site, all with picnic tables and fire rings. There are vault toilets, and potable water is available in season. Sites are suitable for tents, trailers, and RVs. Most sites are reservable in advance, and a few may be available on a first-come, first-served basis. The campground is typically open from spring through fall, depending on snowpack and creek levels.

Photos: https://t2bk.com/ARV

193. COCONINO RIM ROAD DISPERSED CAMPING - FREE

- Coconino Rim Rd.
- Grand Canyon, AZ
- GPS: 35.9623, -111.9644

Map: https://t2bk.com/APS

Very near the Grand Canyon. This superb location is approximately 3 miles away from Grandview Point within the park and close to all the attractions on the South Rim. Elk and deer are often seen roaming through, and birdlife is abundant. The area has established camping spots along the road, which is primarily smooth dirt, except for the initial quarter mile that may have ruts due to wet weather driving. However, during dry weather, any car or RV should be able to travel along it easily.

There are no designated sites, but dispersed camping is permitted along the road in established clearings. No developed facilities are available—no toilets, water, or trash services—so you'll need to pack everything in and out. Many other forest service roads in the Grand Canyon region offer free campsites. Check the resources provided at the end for additional information.

Photos: https://t2bk.com/APT

194. BURNT CORRAL CAMPGROUND - $20/$10

- Tonto National Forest
- FR-183
- Roosevelt, AZ 85545
- GPS: 33.6255, -111.2027

Maps: https://t2bk.com/ARW

Burnt Corral Campground lies along the south shore of Apache Lake in rugged canyon walls and Sonoran Desert terrain. Saguaros, mesquite, and palo verde trees dot the shoreline, and the lake's 17-mile length offers fishing, boating, and water-sport access. The steep canyon walls and clear water create a dramatic backdrop, and you might spot birds such as osprey or javelina roaming the brush. While trails don't start directly from your site, nearby roads lead to overlooks and quiet coves for hiking and photography.

The campground has 76 developed sites, each with a parking spur, picnic table, fire ring with grill, and a shade ramada around the grill. There are vault toilets and potable water spigots throughout the area. Sites are available by reservation for odd-numbered spots, and even-numbered sites operate on a first-come, first-served basis. Open year-round.

Photos: https://t2bk.com/ARX

195. CANYON VIEW CAMPGROUND - FREE

- Canyon View Campground Rd.
- Shonto, AZ
- GPS: 36.687, -110.5417

Map:
https://t2bk.com/APU

Near Monument Valley. This is a well-maintained campground located right behind the Navajo National Monument Visitor Center, which is available for free. The campground has all the necessary amenities, such as tables, grills, trash cans, and clean bathrooms. The spots are serene and well-kept, offering spectacular views of the canyon. The sunrise views from the campground are genuinely awe-inspiring.

There are some excellent hiking opportunities available nearby. Visitors can enjoy short hikes near the visitor center, offering a glimpse of the ancestral villages. Campsites are first-come, first-served. The ground is mostly level gravel or dirt, able to accommodate tents, vans, and small RVs. It is not suitable for bigger rigs. The campground is open most of the year, though seasonal changes may affect access.

Photos:
https://t2bk.com/APV

196. HORSE SPRINGS CAMPGROUND - $16/$8

- Apache-Sitgreaves National Forest
- Rte. 276
- Alpine, AZ 85920
- GPS: 33.7843, -109.3484

Maps: https://t2bk.com/ARY

Horse Springs Campground sits beside the East Fork of the Black River in the White Mountains of Arizona. Tall ponderosa and mixed-conifer forests line the stream, creating a lush, shaded atmosphere at around 7,600 feet elevation. Riparian vegetation and grasses edge the river, and you'll likely spot mule deer, squirrels, and a variety of songbirds. A short nature trail follows the creek, and larger trails into the forest are within driving distance for hiking and exploration.

The campground offers 27 sites, each outfitted with a picnic table, fire ring, and grill. Vault toilets and trash containers are provided, but there is no potable water. Sites are suitable for tents, small trailers, and RVs, and are first-come, first-served—reservations are not accepted. The site is generally open from late spring through fall, depending on snow and road access.

Photos: https://t2bk.com/ARZ

197. SUNSET VIEW CAMPGROUND - FREE

- Navajo National Monument
- AZ-564
- Kayenta, AZ
- GPS: 36.6765, -110.5423

Map: https://t2bk.com/APW

Near Monument Valley. Sunset View Campground is near Kayenta, Arizona, within the high desert landscape of the Navajo Nation. The campground sits on a low mesa with wide, unobstructed views of Monument Valley to the northeast and sun-drenched canyons to the south and west. The land is mostly open, dotted with desert shrubs, scattered junipers, and soft red sandstone underfoot. Sunrises and sunsets are especially dramatic here, with long, flat vistas and distant buttes silhouetted against the sky.

The access is paved, and the sites are split between back-in and "pull-through" shoulder sites along the road. The spots are level, and the views will leave you breathless. First-come, first-served. This spot isn't ideal for big rigs. All sites are first-come, first-served. The campground generally remains open year-round, though usage may ebb during extreme summer heat.

Photos: https://t2bk.com/APX

198. FRAZIER HORSE CAMPGROUND - $16/$8

- Tonto National Forest
- Hwy 188
- Roosevelt, AZ 85545
- GPS: 33.6663, -111.1234

Maps: https://t2bk.com/ASA

Frazier Horse Campground is located along the edge of Rosevelt Lake near Roosevelt, Arizona, surrounded by Sonoran desert terrain and towering lake-carved cliffs. The landscape features grassy washes shifting into desert shrubs, and the nearby trail network, including the start of the Arizona Trail, offers access into open country for horseback riders and hikers alike. Wildlife such as mule deer, coyotes, javelina, and various birds, including eagles, are often seen at daybreak or dusk.

The campground has about 11 equestrian-specific units, each equipped with a picnic table, fire ring, grill, and horse corrals. There are vault toilets and a potable water spigot on-site. Reservations are required for all sites, and trailers must be 32 feet or shorter. The campground is dedicated to horse campers and offers direct trail access from the camp.

Photos: https://t2bk.com/ASB

199. NOLAN DESIGNATED DISPERSED CAMPING - FREE

- Coconino National Forest
- Loy Butte Rd. (Forest Road-525)
- Sedona, AZ
- GPS: 34.883, -111.909

Map: https://t2bk.com/APY

This is part of the West Sedona Designated Dispersed Camping Area. This system will protect natural resources, keep the landscape from being dotted by the creation of dispersed campsites, and still provide many places for visitors to camp and enjoy the beauty of west Sedona. Dispersed camping in these areas is on a first-come, first-served basis. Dispersed camping in west Sedona outside of these eight designated sites is prohibited.

There are 8 other dispersed camping areas along Forest Road-525. Pay attention to the signs, as in some places, camping is not allowed. Fair warning: Dispersed camping in the Sedona area can be crowded and very difficult to find at peak times of the year.

Photos:https://t2bk.com/APZ

200. LUNA LAKE CAMPGROUND - $20/$10

- Apache-Sitgreaves National Forest
- FR-570
- Alpine, AZ 85920
- GPS: 33.8374, -109.0798

Maps: https://t2bk.com/ASC

Luna Lake Campground is approximately 8,000 feet in elevation in a stand of ponderosa pines and meadows near the shore of Luna Lake in eastern Arizona. The lake and adjacent wetland provide good opportunities for trout fishing, calm paddles, and birdwatching; you may spot waterfowl and even bald eagles in the area. Trails and non-motorized paths lead through forest and meadow from the camp, and the open layout offers views of surrounding ridges and sky.

Photos: https://t2bk.com/ASD

The campground has 50 individual sites, plus three group sites. Each individual site offers a picnic table and a fire ring with a grill. Vault toilets are provided, and potable water is available seasonally. Trailers and RVs up to 32 feet can be accommodated. There are no utility hookups. Some sites are reservable while others are first-come, first-served.

201. CIENEGUITA CAMPING AREA - FREE

- Las Cienegas National Conservation Area
- East Yucca Farm Rd.
- Elgin, AZ
- GPS: 31.7661, -110.6282

Map: https://t2bk.com/AQA

Cieneguita Camping Area sits in the rolling grasslands of southern Arizona near Elgin, offering a peaceful desert basin landscape ringed by distant mountain ranges. The area is mostly flat and open, with scattered mesquite and oak trees providing light shade. Wildlife sightings include pronghorn, mule deer, and a variety of bird species, particularly near the nearby cienega wetlands that give the area its name. The Patagonia Mountains and Sonoita Creek are not far off, and the surrounding area includes several unpaved roads suitable for hiking, horseback riding, or dispersed exploration.

This dispersed camping area is undeveloped, with no designated sites, restrooms, or potable water. It's open to tents, vans, and trailers that can handle uneven terrain. There are no established reservations or seasonal closures. It's a quiet spot often used by birders, hikers, and those exploring Las Cienegas National Conservation Area.

Photos; https://t2bk.com/AQB

202. WILLARD SPRINGS ROAD DISPERSED CAMPING - FREE

- Coconino National Forest
- Willard Springs Rd.
- Munds Park, AZ
- GPS: 34.9704, -111.6926

Map: https://t2bk.com/AQC

Peaceful and wild. Beautiful, wooded sites with grass under the trees. A free dispersed camping area in the Coconino National Forest. This is a great camping site with room to spread out. The roads are rough at times, especially during rains, but the areas are large enough to accommodate most any size rig.

This spot is beautiful. It's peaceful and surrounded by wild nature. Gorgeous, wooded sites with grassy patches under the trees. Free dispersed camping area in the Coconino National Forest! There's room to spread out here. Although the roads can be rough during rainy times, the sites are spacious enough to fit just about any rig.

Photos: https://t2bk.com/AQD

FYI: A designated shooting area is nearby, so expect gunshots occasionally. Great cell service.

203. PUMP STATION ROAD DISPERSED CAMPING - FREE

- N. Pump Station Rd.
- Marana, AZ
- GPS: 32.4448, -111.3717

Map: https://t2bk.com/AQE

Caution: There is a 6000 lb. GVWR bridge on Silverbell Rd. To bypass this bridge, access Pump Station Rd. via W. El Tiro Rd.Great boondocking spot with stunning views of mountains and cacti, and it's accessible to big rigs and has good cell service. There's plenty of space between campsites and access to all the necessities you need. While the forest may not be as lush as others, you'll still see saguaros around to remind you that you're in the desert.

If you're up for some exploring, there are some great nearby attractions, including the Arizona-Sonoran Desert Museum, Saguaro National Park (West), and the city of Tucson with its grocery stores and restaurants - all about a 45-minute drive away.

Photos: https://t2bk.com/AQF

204. OLD RIM ROAD DESIGNATED DISPERSED CAMPING - FREE

- Apache-Sitgreaves National Forest
- Old Rim Rd. (FR-171)
- Payson, AZ
- GPS: 34.295, -110.8918

Map: https://t2bk.com/AQG

Old Rim Road Designated Dispersed Camping is along a scenic stretch of the historic General Crook Trail near Payson, Arizona. At over 7,500 feet elevation, this area is dominated by tall ponderosa pines and mixed conifers, with grassy patches and rocky outcrops. The terrain is relatively flat, making it easy to explore on foot. Nearby trails include segments of the Highline National Recreation Trail and several forest service paths. Wildlife sightings may include elk, deer, and wild turkeys.

Old Rim Road is well-maintained, and you'll find large campsites with handmade rock fire pits. Most spots are easy to navigate in and out of, and the remote location offers a peaceful camping experience under a starry night sky. If you're looking for solitude, this is the spot for you. Be aware that no water or toilet facilities are available, so come prepared.

Photos: https://t2bk.com/AQH

205. HORSE CORRAL DISPERSED CAMPING - FREE

- Apache-Sitgreaves National Forest
- FR 249C
- Greer, AZ
- GPS: 33.8654, -109.4293

Map: https://t2bk.com/AQI

Horse Corral Dispersed Camping sits in a forested clearing near the eastern slopes of the White Mountains. Surrounded by tall spruce, fir, and aspen trees, the area offers cool summer shade and access to alpine meadows. Elevation is just over 8,000 feet, and the terrain is mostly flat with a few gentle slopes. Wildlife like elk and mule deer are often seen, especially at dawn or dusk. The nearby West Fork Trail and East Fork Trail follow creeks and connect to longer routes for hikers and anglers alike.

The campsites are spread out in a relatively quiet area off forest roads, with enough space for tents, vans, or small RVs. There are no developed facilities, no restrooms, and no potable water, so you need to be self-sufficient. Open generally late spring through early fall, depending on snow and road conditions. It's a good idea to scout ahead. Sites are not marked or reservable.

Photos: https://t2bk.com/AQJ

206. GUNSIGHT WASH DISPERSED CAMPING - FREE

- BLM
- Highway 85
- Why, AZ
- GPS: 32.2395, -112.7508

Map: https://t2bk.com/AQL

Accessing the site is hassle-free, and you can park rigs of any size. The location gives off a desert community vibe, with ample space for tranquil privacy. You will see many people walking their dogs during the mornings and evenings, cycling during the day, and congregating around campfires at night. There is exceptional cell service in the area. The quiet spot can accommodate many campers and is easy to locate.

Ajo, a town located ten miles north, and the Organ Pipe Cactus National Monument, just a few miles away, are popular attractions. Puerto Peñasco in Mexico is also a reasonable distance. No services are available, and there is no water. A gas station and well-stocked convenience store are nearby. The area is accessible year-round, though summers can be extremely hot. Camping is first-come, first-served.

Photos: https://t2bk.com/AQM

207. HORSESHOE CAMPGROUND - $16/$8

- Tonto National Forest
- Horseshoe Dam Rd. (FR-205A)
- Carefree, AZ
- GPS: 33.9772, -111.7171

Maps: https://t2bk.com/ATO

Horseshoe Campground is set just below the rim of the canyon where the Verde River flows out of Horseshoe Reservoir, surrounded by rugged ridges and open desert terrain. The campground is in a mesquite bosque near the riverbank, with cottonwood trees and patches of shade. The setting is remote, and you'll find short walks to the river's edge and views of soaring hawks and occasionally bald eagles. Wildflowers bloom seasonally, and the quiet of the canyon makes early morning wildlife sightings likely—mule deer often roam the bosques.

There are 12 designated campsites, each with a picnic table and fire ring. Vault toilets are available; there is no potable water or trash service, so you'll need to pack in and pack out. Sites are first-come, first-served only. The campground is open year-round, though access may depend on weather and vehicle clearance.

Photos: https://t2bk.com/ATP

208. PALM CANYON DISPERSED - FREE

- Kofa National Wildlife Refuge
- Palm Canyon Rd.
- Quartzsite, AZ
- GPS: 33.3603, -114.10

Map: https://t2bk.com/AQN

The scenery at this location showcases the beauty of the Arizona desert. Palm Canyon Dispersed Camping sits in a broad, rocky wash just outside Kofa National Wildlife Refuge, south of Quartzsite. The setting is rugged and stark, with desert floor framed by volcanic hills and jagged ridges. Palo verde and creosote provide sparse vegetation, while giant saguaro and ocotillo dot the surrounding hillsides. The Palm Canyon Trail is nearby and leads to a narrow canyon where a rare stand of native California fan palms survives—a short, rocky hike worth the effort.

It's conveniently located near all winter events in Quartzsite, yet far enough away from the crowds to provide a peaceful and calming boondocking experience. There are plenty of flat areas to park vehicles of any size. Open year-round. Camping is first-come, first-served.

Photos: https://t2bk.com/AQO

209. COLOSSAL CAVE MOUNTAIN PARK - $15/$7.50

- County Park
- 16721 E. Old Spanish Trail
- Vail, AZ 85641
- GPS: 32.0624, -110.6343

Maps: https://t2bk.com/ATM

Colossal Cave Mountain Park Campground is tucked into Posta Quemada Canyon near Vail, Arizona, surrounded by saguaros, mesquites, and ponderosa pines. You're close to the southern end of the Arizona Trail and several short hikes, including the Bundrick Trail and Path of the Ancestors, which follow riparian washes and desert slopes. Wildlife you'll likely spot includes jackrabbits, desert birds, and occasionally bobcats or coyotes just at dusk. The canyon offers quiet shade and a desert foothills feel.

The campground has 30 individual campsites scattered along the canyon floor, plus two large group areas. Each campsite has a picnic table, fire ring, and grill. Vault toilets are available, and potable water is from a spigot. Sites can fit tents, vans, and small RVs, and all spots are first-come, first-served. Gates into the campground close at 4 p.m., and access is generally available year-round.

Photos: https://t2bk.com/ATN

210. PLOMOSA ROAD DISPERSED CAMPING - FREE

- BLM
- Plomosa Rd.
- Bouse, AZ
- GPS: 33.748711, -114.215885

Map: https://t2bk.com/AQP

This area can be popular among snowbirds during winter, but you can still find some solitude if that's what you're after. Parker and Quartzite are both about a 30-minute drive in either direction. There are many opportunities to walk in the desert and ride four-wheelers on nearby trails. The area backs up to the mountains, and you'll enjoy breathtaking sunrises and sunsets. The site is quite large, so you can have plenty of space between you and your neighbors. This spot offers wide-open spaces and is friendly to big rigs.

The roads are generally hard-packed, and it's conveniently close to the town of Bouse, where you can find a Dollar Tree, a small grocery store, and a post office. Water, dump, and recycling facilities are located on Plomosa Road.

Photos: https://t2bk.com/AQQ

211. LA POSA TYSON WASH LTVA AND LA POSA SOUTH LTVA - CHEAP LONG TERM STAY IN THE WINTER!

- BLM Long Term Visitor Area
- Highway 95
- Quartzsite, AZ
- GPS: 33.6251, -114.2156

Map: https://t2bk.com/AQR

Affordable with free dump/water/trash! The LTVA long-term permit ($180) allows the use of Bureau of Land Management designated LTVAs continuously from September 15th to April 15th (a total of 7 months), or for any length of time between those dates.

The LTVA short-visit permit ($40) allows using any of the Bureau of Land Management designated LTVAs for 14 consecutive days from September 15th to April 15th, beginning on the day the permit receipt is exchanged for the official permit and decal. The short-visit permit may be renewed an unlimited number of times for the cost of the permit. LTVA permits are valid at all of the Bureau of Land Management LTVA sites.

Photos: https://t2bk.com/AQS

212. IMPERIAL DAM LONG TERM VISITOR AREA - CHEAP LONG TERM STAY IN THE WINTER!

- BLM Long Term Visitor Area
- Senator Wash Rd.
- Winterhaven, CA
- GPS: 32.9013, -114.4962

Map: https://t2bk.com/AQT

Technically, this is in California (by about ½ miles), but access is from Hwy 95 in Arizona. There are thousands of acres to spread out. It's affordable, with free dump/water/trash! The nearby Christian Service Center offers mail and package delivery, propane, and filtered water. The LTVA long-term permit ($180) allows the use of Bureau of Land Management designated LTVAs continuously from September 15th to April 15th (a total of 7 months) or for any length of time between those dates.

The LTVA short-visit permit ($40) allows the use of designated LTVAs for 14 consecutive days from September 15th to April 15th. Permits are valid at all of the Bureau of Land Management LTVAs.

Photos: https://t2bk.com/AQU

12
NEW MEXICO

214. LITTLE ARSENIC SPRINGS CAMPGROUND - $7/$3.50

- Rio Grande del Norte National Monument
- Little Arsenic
- Questa, NM
- GPS: 36.6677, -105.68

Map: https://t2bk.com/AQV

Little Arsenic Springs Campground lies along the rim of the Rio Grande Gorge near the village of Pilar in northern New Mexico. The terrain is dry and open with rocky soil, scattered piñon and juniper, and desert grasses. Views stretch across the gorge to layered cliffs and volcanic mesas. Bighorn sheep are sometimes spotted on the canyon walls, and the Rio Grande flows below with access to fishing, rafting, and trails. The nearby West Rim Trail follows the edge of the canyon and connects to other overlooks and scenic spots along the gorge.

The campground has 5 sites, each with a picnic table and fire ring. Vault toilets are available, but there is no water. Parking is separate from the tent pads, and the area is best suited to tent camping and small RVs under 20ft. Sites are first-come, first-served. The campground is open seasonally, from spring through fall.

Photos: https://t2bk.com/AQW

215. ANGEL PEAK CAMPGROUND - FREE

- BLM
- CR-7175
- Bloomfield, NM 87413
- GPS: 36.5482, -107.8602

Maps:
https://t2bk.com/ASF

Angel Peak Campground is located along the rim of the badlands in the Angel Peak Scenic Area, near Bloomfield, New Mexico. The views are of deep canyons and the sculpted sandstone and mudstone formations falling away beneath the 6,988-foot Angel Peak. A short nature trail winds alongside the rim, offering overlooks and benches from which to view the terrain. Wildlife like lizards, snakes, and small birds forage among the desert scrub and rocks.

This small campground has nine sites, each equipped with a picnic table on a concrete pad, a gravel walkway, a fire grate, and, in some sites, a shade shelter. Two accessible vault toilets and trash receptacles are available. Potable water is not available. The sites are first-come, first-served and open year-round.

Photos:
https://t2bk.com/ASG

216. CEBOLLA MESA CAMPGROUND -FREE

- Carson National Forest
- FR-9
- Questa, NM
- GPS: 36.6405, -105.6891

Map: https://t2bk.com/AQX

Small campground with only five sites. Cebolla Mesa Campground is perched high above the Rio Grande Gorge in northern New Mexico, offering sweeping views of the surrounding mesas and canyonlands. The area is open and exposed, with sparse juniper, sagebrush, and native grasses. The landscape rolls gently toward the canyon rim, where cliffs drop steeply into the gorge below. Mule deer and raptors are common, and the sound of the river may be faintly audible depending on wind and season. The nearby West Rim Trail provides access to hiking with panoramic views.

The campsites have picnic tables and fire rings. Vault toilets are available. There is no water on-site. Sites are first-come, first-served and accessible by most vehicles during dry weather. The campground is typically open from late spring through fall, depending on snow and road conditions.

Photos: https://t2bk.com/AQY

217. NORTHPOINT CAMPGROUND - $20

- Bluewater Lake State Park
- Hwy 412
- Prewitt, NM 87045
- GPS: 35.3023, -108.1073

Maps: https://t2bk.com/ASH

Northpoint Campground sits at about 7,400 feet elevation along the shoreline of Bluewater Lake State Park in New Mexico, surrounded by views of the Zuni Mountains and open lake waters. You'll find a mix of forested patches and open flats, with water access, shoreline walks, and nearby trails for hiking or wildlife spotting — keep an eye out for ducks, raptors, and deer at dusk. The elevated terrain offers wide skies and relatively cool evenings.

The campground includes sites that can accommodate tents, vans, and RVs. Each has a picnic table and a fire ring. Amenities include drinking water, restrooms, and a dump station. Some sites can be reserved in advance; others are available on a first-come, first-served basis. Campsites typically have access year-round.

Photos: https://t2bk.com/ASI

218. LOS PIÑOS CAMPGROUND - FREE

- Carson National Forest
- Los Pinos River Access Rd.
- Tierra Amarilla, NM
- GPS: 36.9544, -106.1706

Map: https://t2bk.com/AQZ

Los Piños Campground is tucked into a scenic canyon near the Rio de los Piños in northern New Mexico, not far from the Colorado border. The campground is surrounded by tall conifers and aspen, offering a cool, shaded escape during summer months. The nearby river provides opportunities for trout fishing and quiet walks along the bank. Elk and deer are sometimes seen in the area, and birdlife is active around the water and forest edges. The surrounding terrain is rugged and forested, with access to nearby trails and back roads.

This is a small, primitive campground with only four sites. Each site includes a picnic table and fire ring, and there is a vault toilet on-site. No potable water is available. The campground is generally open during the warmer months and is first-come, first-served. The setting is remote and peaceful, especially on weekdays.

Photos: https://t2bk.com/ARA

219. BROWN SPRINGS CAMPGROUND - FREE

- Glade Run Recreation Area
- CR-1980
- Farmington, NM 87401
- GPS: 36.8061, -108.1806

Maps: https://t2bk.com/ASJ

Brown Springs Campground is in the Glade Run Recreation Area near Farmington, New Mexico, in a high-desert landscape of sandy washes, slick rock, and sparse pinyon-juniper terrain. The area is ideal for off-road and dual-sport riders with nearby trails, and birdwatchers will spot turkeys, mule deer, and songbirds dotting the scrub and bush. Open skies lend themselves to evening campfires and stargazing.

The developed area offers 10 gravel sites, each with a picnic table and fire ring. A vault toilet is on site, but there is no potable water. Sites accommodate tents, vans, and RVs, and the location is first-come, first-served. A free camping permit is required from the local BLM office before overnighting, and the area is open year-round with potential restrictions during events.

Photos: https://t2bk.com/ASK

220. BLACK CANYON CAMPGROUND - $10/$5

- Santa Fe National Forest
- Hyde Park Road
- Santa Fe, NM
- GPS: 35.7278, -105.8394

Map:
https://t2bk.com/ARB

Black Canyon Campground sits among spruce, aspen, and fir trees at about 8,475 feet elevation, providing a mix of sun and shade beneath a tall forest canopy. You'll find a 1.5-mile loop trail that wraps around the campground into surrounding woods, plus several hiking, biking, and horseback trails nearby. It's also just eight miles northeast of Santa Fe, so you get mountain scenery along with relatively easy access to cultural sites in town. Wildlife like mule deer and various forest birds are often seen in the cooler morning hours.

The campground offers 36 sites for cars, RVs, and tents, including a few walk-in tent-only sites. Every site has a picnic table, fire ring with grill, and lantern post. There are accessible vault toilets, but no potable water. Some sites are reservable, and others first-come, first-served. Seasonal access generally runs from early May through mid-October. Reservations recommended.

Photos:
https://t2bk.com/ARC

221. COCHITI CAMPGROUND - $15/$7.50 - $20/$10

- Army Corps Of Engineers
- 82 Dam Crest Rd.
- Peña Blanca, NM 87041
- GPS: 35.6415, -106.3256

Maps: https://t2bk.com/ASL

Cochiti Campground is along the shores of Cochiti Lake in Sandoval County, New Mexico, at an elevation of around 5,300 feet. This area is juniper and piñon woodlands and mixed grasses, with views of the Jemez Mountains rising on the horizon. A network of natural walking paths skirts the lake and leads toward osprey nesting platforms and the shoreline, and you'll frequently spot mule deer, coyotes, rabbits, and various birds hunting or perching atop nearby ridges.

Photos: https://t2bk.com/ASM

The campground has four loops offering approximately 65 sites, including water-and-electric-hookup units and non-electric tent-friendly sites. Each site has a picnic table, fire ring, and grill. There are restrooms, showers, water spigots, and a dump station for larger rigs. *** All sites are reservation-only—

first-come-first-served is not an option—and the facility is managed year-round by the U.S. Army Corps of Engineers.

222. JUNIPER FAMILY CAMPGROUND - $20/$10

- Bandelier National Monument
- NM-4
- Los Alamos, NM
- GPS: 35.7954, -106.2794

Map: https://t2bk.com/ARD

Juniper Family Campground is located just inside the entrance of Bandelier National Monument, on the Pajarito Plateau. You're surrounded by piñon-juniper woodlands and high desert terrain with some ponderosa pines; trails like Frijoles Canyon and the Frey Trail begin nearby, offering hikes through canyon vistas and access to archaeological sites. Wildlife you might see includes mule deer, forest birds, and small mammals.

There are 53 individual campsites plus 2 group sites divided among three loops: Abert's Squirrel Loop (Loop A), Black Bear Loop (Loop B), and Coyote Loop (Loop C). Each site has a picnic table, fire ring with grill, food locker, and paved parking pull-in or pull-through. Flush toilets and water spigots are found at comfort stations in each loop. Some sites can be reserved in advance; others are available first-come, first-served. The campground is open wherever seasonal access permits.

Photos: https://t2bk.com/ARE

223. HERON LAKE STATE PARK - $20/$15

- New Mexico State Park
- Highway 95
- Los Ojos, NM 87551
- GPS: 36.694, -106.657

Maps:
https://t2bk.com/ASN

Heron Lake State Park is in northern New Mexico, surrounded by pine and spruce forests. The lake is a no-wake zone, ideal for quiet boating, kayaking, and paddleboarding. Wildlife is abundant, with osprey nests nearby, bald eagles are frequently seen, and mule deer roam the area. The Rio Chama Trail connects the park to the nearby river gorge via a pedestrian suspension bridge, offering scenic hiking through meadows and woods.

The park includes over 190 campsites, ranging from primitive shoreline spots to developed sites with electric hookups. There are restrooms, showers, drinking water, and a dump station. Most sites have picnic tables and fire rings. Some areas are reservable while others are first-come, first-served. Sites can accommodate tents and RVs of various sizes. The campground is generally open year-round, with the most popular season running late spring through early fall.

Photos:
https://t2bk.com/ASO

224. OLIVER LEE MEMORIAL STATE PARK CAMPGROUND - $20/$30

- New Mexico State Parks
- 409 Dog Canyon Rd.
- Alamogordo, NM
- GPS: 32.7474, -105.9147

Map: https://t2bk.com/ARF

This stunning state park campground is near White Sands National Park. The landscape is Chihuahuan Desert—mesquite, yucca, ocotillo, and creosote cover much of the higher flats, while cottonwoods, ferns, and springs line Dog Canyon with more lush growth. A trail begins at the visitor center and climbs Dog Canyon far up toward ridge-tops, and a nature trail follows the riparian area under cottonwoods.

There are 39 campsites, several of which have water and electric hookups (30-amp and one 50-amp ADA site), while the rest are non-electric. Sites have picnic tables and fire rings, with restrooms and showers available. First-come, first-served. Open year-round, with peak use from fall through spring.

Photos: https://t2bk.com/ARG

225. OVERLOOK CAMPGROUND - $9/$4.50

- Santa Cruz Lake Recreation Area
- Cundiyo Road
- Santa Fe, NM 87506
- GPS: 35.9647, -105.9185

Maps: https://t2bk.com/ASP

Overlook Campground sits on a high escarpment at the south end of Santa Cruz Lake Recreation Area near Chimayó, New Mexico. The landscape has wide panoramic views across the lake and surrounding mesas, with sagebrush and scattered juniper lining the rim. The 6.4-mile trail system—including the Overlook Trail—begins nearby and offers moderate hikes through the terrain. Wildlife such as hawks, rabbits, and rattlesnakes are sometimes seen in the open terrain.

The campground offers twelve marked sites, each with a picnic table, shaded shelter, fire ring, or grill. A vault toilet is available on-site, and trash receptacles are provided. There is no potable water at the campground. Sites are first-come, first-served. The access road is unpaved and can be rough in spots, though no special equipment is required in dry conditions.

Photos: https://t2bk.com/ASQ

226. SUNSET REEF CAMPGROUND - FREE

- Near Carlsbad Caverns National Park
- BLM
- Washington Ranch Rd.
- Carlsbad, NM
- GPS: 32.1095, -104.4253

Map: https://t2bk.com/ARH

Sunset Reef Campground is close to the national park, making it a popular choice for visitors. The surrounding flat terrain is mostly open desert with few trees, giving wide views of the Guadalupe Mountains and Carlsbad Caverns off to the north. The night skies are dark, stars are visible, and wildlife such as jackrabbits and desert birds frequent the area. The quality of light at sunrise and sunset makes this a popular stop for photographers and travelers rolling between the parks.

There are 11 developed campsites: five pull-through RV spaces and six tent-or-car sites. Each site includes a shaded picnic table, a fire pit, and a grill. A vault toilet is available, but there is no potable water. All sites are first-come, first-served. The campground is open year-round.

Photos: https://t2bk.com/ARI

227. MILLS CANYON RIM CAMPGROUND - FREE

- Kiowa National Grassland
- Mills Canyon Rd.
- Mills, NM 87730
- GPS: 36.0706, -104.3489

Maps: https://t2bk.com/ASR

Mills Canyon Rim Campground is located at about 5,760 feet in elevation along the rim of the Canadian River Canyon in northeastern New Mexico. It's in a wide-open short-grass prairie that drops dramatically into the canyon, with juniper and scattered pinyon pine near the rim. While there are no formal trails at the campground itself, old ranch tracks and canyon rim routes offer excellent hiking and exploration, and mule deer and raptors are common throughout the grasslands and cliff edges.

The campground has six camp sites, each equipped with a picnic table, fire ring, and grill. Vault toilets are provided, but there is no potable water available. Sites are first-come, first-served. The road to the rim is maintained, though care is advisable when towing larger trailers.

Photos: https://t2bk.com/ASS

228. AGUIRRE SPRING CAMPGROUND - FREE

- Organ Mountains-Desert Peaks National Monument
- Aguirre Springs Rd.
- Las Cruces, NM
- GPS: 32.3704, -106.5609

Map: https://t2bk.com/ARJ

This lovely little campground may not be suitable for larger RVs, but it's an excellent option for those seeking a quiet, peaceful getaway. Tucked away in the high desert, this hidden gem offers stunning views of the nearby peaks on one side and the vista views of White Sands on the other. The entrance road is not recommended for RVs over 23 ft. in length.

It's the perfect spot for visitors who want to feel isolated and surrounded by nature while being close enough to Las Cruces and White Sands for easy access to amenities and attractions. The area offers plenty of opportunities for hiking in the nearby Organ Mountains. Entrance gate hours: March - Nov. 7 AM - 8 PM and Nov. - March: 8 AM - 6 PM.

Photos: https://t2bk.com/ARK

229. NORTH AREA CAMPGROUND - $15/$20

- Conchas Lake State Park
- 501 Bell Ranch Rd.
- Conchas, NM 88416
- GPS: 35.4276, -104.1913

Maps: https://t2bk.com/AST

North Area Campground at Conchas Lake State Park sits along the shoreline of one of New Mexico's larger lakes. You'll find gently rolling terrain with sagebrush and scattered junipers leading down toward the water's edge, and boating access with shoreline walks and bird-watching. Watch for waterfowl and raptors visiting the lake, and you can explore shallow coves or old ranch roads nearby.

The campground features both electric- and non-electric-hookup loops: roughly 24 water-and-electric sites and several non-electric sites. Each site has a picnic table and a fire ring. There are restrooms and a dump station, with potable water available. Reservations are accepted for many sites; others may be first-come. The campground is open year-round and is suitable for both tent campers and RVs.

Photos: https://t2bk.com/ASU

230. CITY OF ROCKS STATE PARK - $15/$30

- New Mexico State Park
- 327 Hwy 61
- Faywood, NM
- GPS: 32.588, -107.9746

Map: https://t2bk.com/ARL

The City of Rocks State Park campground is surrounded by dramatic volcanic spires rising as high as forty feet, creating winding "lanes" between them and giving the park its name. The pinnacles are set in Chihuahuan-desert terrain with scattered shrubs, grasses, and occasional juniper trees. Hiking and biking trails thread through the rocks; the Table Mountain, Hydra, and Cienega trails are nearby. Wildlife includes desert songbirds and small mammals that use the rock cover, and after dark, the park becomes a dark-sky destination for stargazing.

There are 52 campsites, some with electric and water hookups, and others more rustic. Each site is equipped with a picnic table and fire ring. The campground has restrooms and hot showers, and potable water is available. Some campsites are reservable in advance; others are first-come, first-served. The park is open year-round, with more limited services in the off-season.

Photos: https://t2bk.com/ARM

231. SAN JON VILLAGE CAMPGROUND - FREE

- City Park
- Oak Ave.
- San Jon, NM 88434
- GPS: 35.1075, -103.3317

Maps: https://t2bk.com/ASV

South Jon Village Campground is located in a city park in San Jon, New Mexico. It is on flat, open land with short grass and mature shade trees in a small community setting between Interstate 40 and US Route 66. While there are no trails in the park itself, you'll find wide sidewalks and paths for gentle walks, and local birdlife like robins and sparrows can be seen among the trees and shrubs.

The campground offers eight gravel pads suitable for modern RVs and trailers, each with a picnic table and grill. Restrooms with flush toilets are available on-site, and drinking water spigots are provided. Sites are first-come, first-served, and no reservations are taken. The ease of access from both the Interstate and Route 66 makes it a convenient and interesting overnight stop.

Photos: https://t2bk.com/ASW

232. SOUTH MONTICELLO CAMPGROUND - $10/$30

- Elephant Butte Lake State Park
- Monticello Road
- Truth or Consequences, NM
- GPS: 33.2946, -107.1869

Map: https://t2bk.com/ARP

South Monticello Campground is located on the shores of Elephant Butte Reservoir at an elevation of about 4,494 feet. You'll see wide water views, open desert terrain, and nearby ridgelines rising in the distance. The lake attracts waterfowl and shore birds, and deer are spotted along the edges. Trails and haul roads near the campground provide routes for walking, biking, and exploring the arid landscapes.

The campground has 132 sites, many of which provide both water and electric hookups. Each site includes a picnic table, fire ring, and gravel pad. There are flush restrooms and hot showers on site, plus a dump station. All sites are reservable in advance. The campground is open year-round.

Photos: https://t2bk.com/ARO

233. RIO FERNANDO DE TAOS DISPERSED CAMPING - FREE

- Carson National Forest
- FR-5
- Angel Fire, NM 87710
- GPS: 36.4225, -105.3423

Maps: https://t2bk.com/ASX

Rio Fernando de Taos Dispersed Camping sits along a scenic canyon section in the forest near Taos, New Mexico. Camping is amid piñon and juniper woodlands, with open overlooks that drop into tight chasms, and views to distant mountain peaks. Nearby trails follow the river and ridge-tops, offering moderate hikes and views of sweeping vistas. Wildlife sightings often include mule deer, hawks circling overhead, and small mammals scurrying through the brush.

Camping is in clearings along the forest road. There are no marked pads, restrooms, or potable water, so you need to be completely self-contained. Both tents and RVs can find space, though some sites suit smaller rigs best. Spots operate on a first-come, first-served basis. The access road is maintained, and summer through early fall are the most accessible seasons.

Photos: https://t2bk.com/ASY

234. COSMIC CAMPGROUND - FREE

- **Cosmic Campground International Dark Sky Sanctuary**
- Gila National Forest
- U.S. 180
- Glenwood, NM
- GPS: 33.4807, -108.92

Map: https://t2bk.com/ARQ

This one gets rave reviews from campers!! Cosmic Campground International Dark Sky Sanctuary (CCIDSS) is the first International Dark Sky Sanctuary located on National Forest System lands and North America.

A fantastic place for stargazing enthusiasts! It's a great spot to witness the beauty of the night sky without any interference from light pollution. However, campers need to respect the dark sky atmosphere by arriving and setting up camp before dusk, using red lights or filters to minimize the impact of artificial light, and avoiding campfires or bright lights that may disrupt the environment. No parking, camping, or campfires are allowed on the observation/telescope pads, and generator use is prohibited from 10 PM - 6 AM.

Photos: https://t2bk.com/ARR

235. SIERRA VISTA DISPERSED CAMPING - FREE

- Organ Mountains-Desert Peaks National Monument
- Dripping Springs Rd.
- Las Cruces, NM 88001
- GPS: 32.3232, -106.6304

Maps: https://t2bk.com/ATQ

Sierra Vista Dispersed Camping near Organ Mountains-Desert Peaks National Monument is set in open Chihuahuan Desert terrain with a backdrop of jagged granite spires. The landscape includes scattered creosote and desert shrubs, wide skies, and distant mountain ridges. Trails like the Sierra Vista Trail are nearby and provide access to the hills for hiking or mountain biking. Wildlife in the area includes jackrabbits, roadrunners, and raptors cruising the ridges.

This dispersed camping area offers informal sites on BLM land—pull-outs and clearings along dirt roads suitable for tents, vans, and trailers. There are no marked pads, restrooms, or drinking water available. Camping is first-come, first-served. Although access roads are generally passable, check current conditions before your arrival.

Photos: https://t2bk.com/ATR

236. CLAYTON LAKE STATE PARK CAMPGROUND - $15

- New Mexico State Park
- 141 Clayton Lake Rd.
- Clayton, NM 88415
- GPS: 36.574, -103.3006

Maps: https://t2bk.com/ATD

Clayton Lake State Park lies on the high plains of northeastern New Mexico, surrounded by rolling grasslands, volcanic rock outcrops, and sandstone cliffs. The lake provides calm waters for fishing and paddling, which is especially popular from spring through fall. You'll find a short boardwalk trail leading to the famous dinosaur trackways exposed in the spillway, and raptors and waterfowl are common around the shore and wetlands.

The campground is in several loops and has about 26 campsites with a mix of standard, water-only, and water-with-electric setups. The campsites have picnic tables and fire rings. There are restrooms with flush toilets and showers, plus potable water at spigots. Reservations are accepted for many sites, while others are on a first-come, first-served basis. The park is open year-round, with full services during the warmer season.

Photos: https://t2bk.com/ATC

237. SUMNER LAKE STATE PARK CAMPGROUND - $8 - $18

- New Mexico State Park
- 32 Lake View Dr.
- Lake Sumner, NM 88119
- GPS: 34.6123, -104.3951

Maps: https://t2bk.com/ATI

Sumner Lake State Park Campground sits along a large lake surrounded by gently rolling grasslands and scrub brush. The shore stretches widely, and the water's edge is accessible from multiple loops. Birdlife and waterfowl populate the shallows, while raptors and deer appear on the surrounding terrain. A lakeside trail links view-points and the visitor center, and boating, paddling, and shoreline walks are popular. Wildlife you may notice includes ducks, geese, and various wading birds, especially near inlets.

The campground has 50 developed sites. Some sites offer hookups (water and electric, $14 to $18), and others are basic spots ($8 to $10). Each has a picnic table and a fire ring. Flush toilets, showers, potable water spigots, and a dump station are provided. Reservations are accepted for many sites; the park is open year-round.

Photos: https://t2bk.com/ATJ

238. YUCCA CAMPGROUND - $10 - $14

- Ute Lake State Park
- State Park Rd.
- Logan, NM 88426
- GPS: 35.3552, -103.4484

Maps: https://t2bk.com/ATK

Yucca Campground at Ute Lake State Park sits beside the 13-mile reservoir on the Canadian River in eastern New Mexico. Campsites on open, mostly level terrain with long views across the water and shores edged by grasses and sagebrush. Boating access, shoreline walks, and bird watching are all right at your campsite, and you'll often spot waterfowl and fish jumping in the shallows. Trails near the visitor center head toward dunes and the lake's edge with quiet natural stretches.

The campground has 45 sites, many of which are pull-through and accommodate trailers, tents, or large RVs. Electric and water hookups are available at most pads. Restrooms are provided, and potable water is supplied within the loop. Reservations are accepted and advised, especially in high season, but some sites may be first-come, first-served. The park remains open year-round with services fully available during peak months.

Photos: https://t2bk.com/ATL

13

RESOURCES

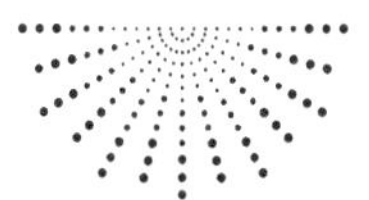

RESOURCES FOR THOUSANDS OF GREAT PLACES TO CAMP

These three are my go-to sites and apps to discover places to camp. I highly recommend further research on any camping area to get the latest info on seasonal closing, road or firc damage, etc.

www.campendium.com

Campendium.com is a comprehensive online resource designed for camping and RV enthusiasts to find, review, and share information about campgrounds and RV parks across the United States and Canada. You'll find detailed campground information, photos, reviews, and a convenient mobile app.

www.freecampsites.net

Freecampsites.net is an online resource that helps campers, and RVers find free and low-cost campsites across the United States and Canada. The platform offers a user-generated database of campgrounds, including reviews, GPS coordinates, and essential information to facilitate budget-friendly camping experiences.

www.ioverlander.com

iOverlander.com is a global online platform and mobile app designed for overlanders, campers, and travelers to find and share information about accommodations, camping spots, points of interest, and essential services, fostering a collaborative community for adventure-seekers worldwide.

GOVERNMENT WEBSITES FOR FURTHER RESEARCH

BLM - Bureau of Land Management www.blm.gov

U.S. Forest Service www.fs.usda.gov

Reserve America www.reserveamerica.com

Recreation.gov www.recreation.gov

Discount Passes https://store.usgs.gov/senior-annual

14

THANK YOU

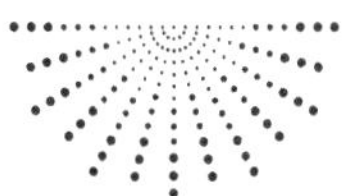

Click or Scan to hear about my next free and cheap camping book. https://amzn.to/44VJ5EG

I HOPE you have enjoyed this book and that it has given you a good idea of the vast choices you'll have in finding beautiful, secluded locations to camp on public land. Choices that won't break the bank. Choices that mean you can camp longer while spending less money. Thank you for reading. I hope you can get out there soon and have some new adventures!

To get notified when my next "free and cheap camping" book is available on Amazon, click the "Follow" button on the linked page above.

Please leave a review on Amazon!

LEAVE A REVIEW!

Enjoying this Book? Please leave a review:

Leave a review: https://t2bk.com/ATU

FREE AND SUPER CHEAP CAMPING SERIES

The Free and Super Cheap Camping series is your passport to budget-friendly adventures across America's most beautiful public lands in:

COLORADO, UTAH, NEVADA, CALIFORNIA, OREGON, WASHINGTON, ARIZONA, NEW MEXICO

Each book features top-rated campsites, plus the tools and knowledge to help you discover thousands more. Whether you're camping in the mountains, by the sea, or in the desert, you'll find detailed information, GPS coordinates, maps, and tips to help you explore with confidence — all while keeping your travel costs low and your sense of freedom high.

SCAN OR CLICK BELOW TO SEE THE ENTIRE SERIES, AND START PLANNING YOUR NEXT CAMPING ADVENTURE.

Free and Super Cheap Camping Series: https://t2bk.com/ATT

www.ingramcontent.com/pod-product-compliance
Lightning Source LLC
LaVergne TN
LVHW010647110826
845149LV00014B/2985

* 9 7 9 8 9 8 9 7 4 2 0 7 3 *